W9-CHV-033

THE VIOLENT MIND

MARGARET O. HYDE & ELIZABETH HELD FORSYTH, M.D.

THE

VIOLENT MIND

Franklin Watts
New York London Toronto Sydney

Diagrams by Vantage Art

Library of Congress Cataloging-in-Publication Data

Hyde, Margaret O. (Margaret Oldroyd), 1917–
The violent mind / by Margaret O. Hyde and Elizabeth Held Forsyth.
p.   cm.
Includes bibliographical references and index.
Summary: Discusses the biological roots of violence, how it can
reflect a troubled mind, and how such mental problems can be
prevented or treated.
ISBN 0-531-11060-5
1. Violence—United States—Psychological aspects.   2. Violence—
United States.   [1. Violence.]   I. Title.
RC569.5.V55H94   1991
616.85'82—dc20   91-18566 CIP AC

CONTENTS

The substance of the vignettes in this book, when not based on actual cases, is rooted in reality. Some are composites, and in some cases, just a name has been changed to provide anonymity.

1
YOUTH AND VIOLENCE

Twelve-year-old David Opont was walking home from school when the neighborhood bully demanded his money. When David refused to hand it over, he was taken to a deserted basement and told to lie on the floor. David's attacker searched him and then pressed a burning object against his back. Finally, he tied David to a pole and set him on fire. Although he was in great pain, David broke free and ran for help. He had third-degree burns over more than half of his body before men at a nearby auto body shop were able to snuff out the flames. Listed in critical condition the day after the ordeal, David suffered severely during the following months. His skin was permanently damaged, and he may never be able to participate in sports. Therapists have helped him to deal with the emotional scars.[1]

David's attacker was only thirteen years old. How could he be so violent? And why? These questions are asked many times in many neighborhoods throughout the United States. They are questions that make the exploration of the causes and prevention of violence increasingly important. They are questions that motivate people to learn more about violent minds.

In David's case, the thirteen-year-old boy who treated him

9

so viciously was a lonely and troubled foster child who had a reputation for beating up other children and extorting money from them. After dropping out of school, where his learning disabilities were an extra handicap, he spent his days wandering around the streets and playing video games at his foster home. This bully had often been attacked by older boys, who thought he was weird. They laughed at his strange behavior, which included collecting, then beating, stray dogs, chasing a younger boy with a dead cat, and running nude across a rooftop. Setting fire to another human being was not his first display of violence.

In another neighborhood where gunfire and street violence are common, fifteen-year-old Varsey was shot and killed for what seemed like less reason than David's refusal to give up his money. Varsey's tragedy began after arguments that were based on his "dissing" a boy who belonged to another group of teens. In street language, dissing means refusing to slap hands with someone, an action that shows disrespect. In Varsey's case, it also meant death.

CITY AND COUNTRY VIOLENCE

Violence in New York City is at a level that would have been unimaginable a generation ago. Washington, D.C., has been called the murder capital of the United States, and Los Angeles is famous for its gangs. In Boston, Philadelphia, Houston, Chicago, and other large cities, murders have escalated at an alarming rate.[2] The bar graph on page 11 shows the rising homicide rate in five large cities. Random killings, drive-by shootings, and cold-blooded executions have made many city residents live with fear and anxiety on a daily basis. Many inner-city children are faced with the loss of a close family member, a situation that may lead to violence when their grief is unresolved. At best, it can interfere drastically with their normal ability to learn.

There are whole sections of urban America in which murder, mayhem, and drug overdose have become routine, and the innocent who walk among violent youths know that those arrested return to the streets to repeat their violent attacks in what seems like a revolving-door system of justice. In many neigh-

10

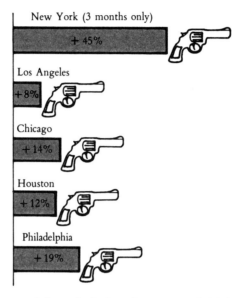

The Rising Homicide Rate

Change in homicides between the first six months of 1989 and the first six months of 1990.

New York (3 months only)

+ 45%

Los Angeles

+ 8%

Chicago

+ 14%

Houston

+ 12%

Philadelphia

+ 19%

New York's figure includes 87 deaths from the Bronx social club fire; without them, the increase would be 22 percent.

Source: *Police departments*

borhoods, the nights are filled with the noise of automatic and semiautomatic weapon fire and the sirens of police cars and ambulances.

Ten-year-old Deenie lives in an atmosphere of violence every day. She is afraid to take the same route home from school that she took last year. Now she walks an extra block to avoid passing the crack house where her friend Jesse was shot. The news reports called Jesse a mushroom, a name given to someone unwittingly caught in the crossfire of a gun battle between crack dealers. (Bystanders who are hit in the crossfire are called mushrooms because they spring up the way mush-

11

rooms do.) Deenie thinks this is a terrible way to describe a gentle, caring friend.

Everyone in Deenie's neighborhood complains about the noise of frequent shootings. They march with signs that say "Stop the Violence," but it continues. Many people are afraid to watch television at night while sitting near a window of their own apartment.

Violence to and by the young occurs in cities and in the countryside. Although there is not the same degree of violence in rural communities as in urban centers, the image of rural children leading wholesome, trouble-free lives may be far from realistic. As the table on page 13 illustrates, your chance of being a victim of violence and crime is greater if you live in a city, lower if you live in the suburbs, and lowest if you live in a rural area.[3] But the fear of violent crime affects people wherever they live.

HOW MUCH VIOLENCE?

Homicide is the second leading cause of death for all fifteen-to-twenty-four-year-olds in the entire United States. It is also the fourth leading cause of death for one-to-four-year-olds and five-to-fourteen-year-olds.[4] Recent increases in the amount of murder, aggravated assault, rape, and robbery are evident when one looks at the charts on pages 14 through 18.[5]

The Crime Clock on page 19 shows the volume of crime that occurs over brief periods of time. This diagram does not mean that there is, for instance, one violent crime committed during every 19-second period. There may be many more crimes at some times and less at others. The clock represents only an average, but it does give a nationwide view of reported crimes.[6]

With the exception of murder, a great many crimes go unreported. However, statistics for crimes that are reported provide an assessment of the locations and types of crime from which trends can be derived. National and local surveys provide a further overview.

Victimization Rates for Persons Age 12 and Older

Place of residence and population	Crimes of violence	Crimes of theft
Total all areas	31	77
All central cities	43	92
50,000 – 249,999	38	90
250,000–499,999	39	85
500,000–999,999	48	105
1,000,000 or more	48	90
All suburban areas	29	82
50,000–249,999	25	72
250,000–499,999	30	79
500,000–999,999	30	88
1,000,000 or more	33	93
Nonmetropolitan areas	22	58

Note: Rates are per 1,000 population age 12 and older. The population range categories shown under the "all central cities" and "all suburban areas" headings are based only on the size of the central city and do not include the population of the entire metropolitan area.

Persons who live in central cities are more likely than suburban or rural residents to be victimized.

Source: *Report to the Nation on Crime and Justice: Second Edition.* Bureau of Justice Statistics, U.S. Department of Justice, 1988.

WHY IS VIOLENCE INCREASING?

Experts agree that violence will increase in the nineties. Law enforcement agents suggest some answers for this increase, such as continuing wars among drug dealers combined with the easy availability of lethal weapons. They believe that perhaps violence has grown more vicious because of an increase in the disregard for human life.

13

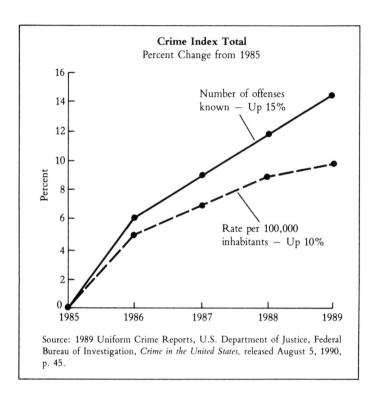

Crime Index Total
Percent Change from 1985

Number of offenses known — Up 15%

Rate per 100,000 inhabitants — Up 10%

Source: 1989 Uniform Crime Reports, U.S. Department of Justice, Federal Bureau of Investigation, *Crime in the United States,* released August 5, 1990, p. 45.

Numerous reports indicate that the amount of violence overall is increasing and that it will continue to do so. Within a short period of time, New York newspapers tell of a kidnapping by a drug gang, the rape of a twelve-year-old girl who was tortured with a heated knife and an ice pick, and the crushing to death of a woman who fell under a van when the occupants wrested a purse from her grasp. Heavily armed gangs roam through large cities, torturing and murdering their victims.

To find out how much violence a young child is exposed to in a typical large city, a report in the October 27, 1987 *Wall Street Journal* chronicled the life of one eleven-year-old, named Lafayette Walton, over a period of three months. Lafayette witnessed gun battles almost daily in his Chicago housing project.

14

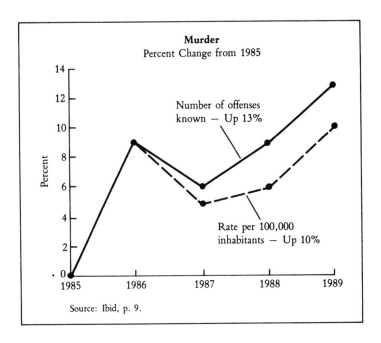

Murder
Percent Change from 1985

Number of offenses
known — Up 13%

Rate per 100,000
inhabitants — Up 10%

Source: Ibid, p. 9.

The violence around him included beatings of relatives and friends, rapes, gang recruiting, cocaine running by a nine-year-old cousin, and several murders.[7]

Younger and younger children are carrying handguns and automatic weapons. Younger and younger children are committing acts of violence and falling victim to the violence of their peers.[8]

The dramatic rise in violence among the young in recent years has shocked and outraged the nation. Teens are twice as likely as adults to be victims of violent crimes and ten times more likely than the elderly. About 45 percent of teen victims recognized or knew the offender. The violence is predominantly intraracial: 83 percent of black teen victims report black assailants, and 76 percent of white teen victims report being attacked by whites. And overall, teens are less likely to report violence than are adults.[9]

15

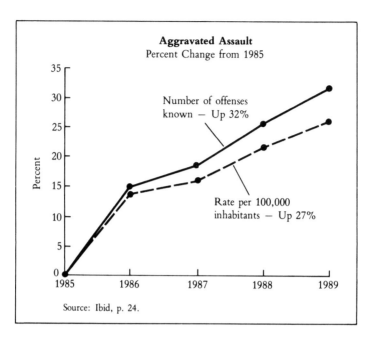

Aggravated Assault
Percent Change from 1985

Number of offenses
known — Up 32%

Rate per 100,000
inhabitants — Up 27%

Source: Ibid, p. 24.

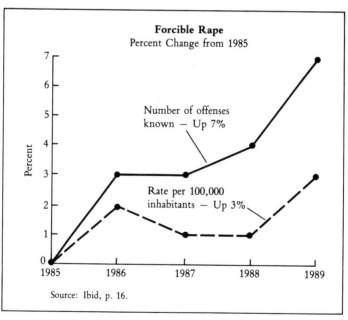

Forcible Rape
Percent Change from 1985

Number of offenses
known — Up 7%

Rate per 100,000
inhabitants — Up 3%

Source: Ibid, p. 16.

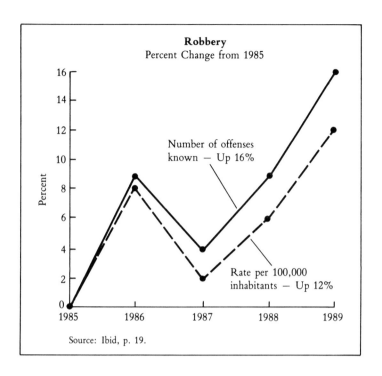

Robbery
Percent Change from 1985

Number of offenses
known — Up 16%

Rate per 100,000
inhabitants — Up 12%

Source: Ibid, p. 19.

WHAT CAUSES VIOLENCE?

Most young people are not violent and do not want to live in a world with violence, but for some of them, violence works, at least in the short term. They think that robbery is a good way to get a new pair of sneakers or a radio. They use violence to get adult attention, respect from their friends, or a gold chain. These young people join violent gangs because they feel that there is no other choice.

Violent rage based on uncontrollable anger may be the result of brain injury, intoxication caused by street drugs such as PCP, or a neurological disease. Triggered by a trivial event, a violent rage can build into an explosion in an instant. Ordinary anger is part of human nature, and the reasons for it are usually apparent, but rage that is linked to brain damage is out of character. People swept up in this kind of rage are embarrassed

17

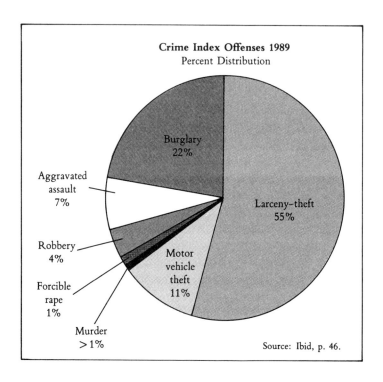

Crime Index Offenses 1989
Percent Distribution

Burglary 22%

Aggravated assault 7%

Larceny–theft 55%

Robbery 4%

Motor vehicle theft 11%

Forcible rape 1%

Murder >1%

Source: Ibid, p. 46.

by it afterward. In cases of normal anger, people feel that they were justified in their behavior. Not all cases of explosive rage result from organic problems, but it is one of the causes of violence that is gaining recognition.[10]

Some young people use violence to satisfy a craving for excitement. Twelve-year-old Cindy is one example. She grew up in a relatively safe suburban neighborhood, but she was a devious manipulator of people. One day she tossed a two-year-old boy into a neighbor's swimming pool because the child would not stop pestering her. Then she watched him struggle until he drowned. When she was sure he was dead, she went to the opposite side of the house to sun herself. After the tragedy was discovered, she lied about what had happened. Although she expressed shock and horror at the "accident," she did not really feel sorry. Cindy actually experienced some pleasure in what she

18

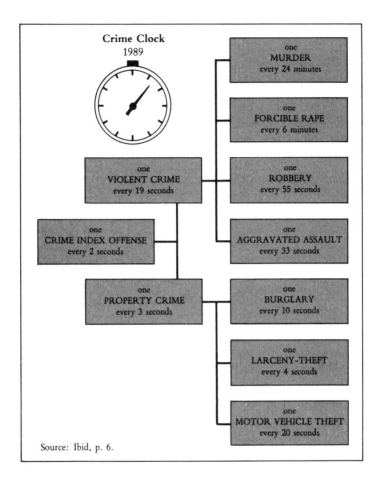

Crime Clock
1989

one
MURDER
every 24 minutes

one
FORCIBLE RAPE
every 6 minutes

one
VIOLENT CRIME
every 19 seconds

one
ROBBERY
every 55 seconds

one
CRIME INDEX OFFENSE
every 2 seconds

one
AGGRAVATED ASSAULT
every 33 seconds

one
PROPERTY CRIME
every 3 seconds

one
BURGLARY
every 10 seconds

one
LARCENY-THEFT
every 4 seconds

one
MOTOR VEHICLE THEFT
every 20 seconds

Source: Ibid, p. 6.

had done, for she had been bored all summer and she enjoyed the excitement.

What caused Cindy to commit such a violent act is a difficult question to answer. It may be easier to explain why violence thrives among children who grow up in "rougher" neighborhoods where acts of brutality are common. Yet why do some children who grow up in the worst of circumstances manage to survive with healthy minds?

Many young people manage to resist peer pressure to use

and sell drugs. They work in fast-food restaurants, join athletic programs, or participate in special training that helps them resist the crowd. But in many neighborhoods, it takes a special courage to resist gangs, drugs, and the violence of the streets.[11]

VIOLENCE YESTERDAY AND TODAY

Although much remains to be learned about why some people can resist the lure of violence and why others cannot, we do know that violence in humans is not new. The story of Cain and Abel and the very beginnings of recorded history tell of violent human minds. Adolescents have long been associated with violent feelings, many of which they do not comprehend. In the famous book *Huckleberry Finn,* Huck becomes a member of Tom Sawyer's gang. The business of the gang is stated as robbery and murder, but this was a nineteenth-century fantasy. Today many adolescent fantasies of violence have become reality. Today's teenagers are victims and perpetrators in the world of violent crime in disproportionate numbers, so it is not surprising that arrest rates for serious crimes are highest in the younger age groups.[12]

Reports of gang rapes and other assaults by teens have grown all too common, but only a small number reach the news media. The following case received special attention because of its viciousness and because it typified the new word—wilding—an activity that occurs when young people are looking for something to do. The teens who beat and raped a young woman jogger in New York's Central Park on a clear spring night in 1989 began as a group of about thirty-five boys who set out to make mischief that evening. After roaming the park and attempting to attack several individuals, the number of boys dwindled. Only seven boys remained as the group that did the most brutal violence.

This bloodthirsty attack of April 1989 has been well publicized, perhaps because the victim was a white woman with degrees from Wellesley and Yale. The location of the crime, Central Park, the viciousness of the attack, and the coining of

20

the word *wilding* all may have had a part in gaining national attention for this particular crime. Those who read about the way this band of seven black and Hispanic teens chased the twenty-eight-year-old investment banker into a gully, beat her senseless with a rock and a metal pipe, raped her, and left her for dead were made more aware of the violence that can occur without apparent reason.

Long after the attack, newspapers reported the victim's progress as she emerged from a coma and tried to regain her memory. Long after the attack, experts were searching for explanations.

In the first reports, the boys who committed this violence were described as members of apparently stable families. Some of them were known to be caring of neighbors, and it was thought that only one had been in trouble with the law. Still, the police described these attackers as smug and remorseless. They offered only one reason for their actions: escape from boredom. It was something to do. It was fun. Many people asked: "What was in their minds? Is the United States breeding a generation of merciless children?"

As studies of the Central Park incident continued, questions into the early backgrounds of these boys brought to light the fact that a number of them had been involved in other attacks. Some researchers suggested that they either had been victims of abuse themselves or had witnessed terrible violence as children.

Some behavior experts pointed out that the power of a group can lead to actions that an individual would never consider alone. As an individual in the group, each may feel free of accountability. In each mind, there is a need to equal the action of the others, and the frenzy can accelerate as they goad each other to commit violence. This "mob psychology" appears to protect them against remorse. According to some psychologists, attacking people who seem to personify a level of affluence that is unattainable is a common pattern in such group assaults.[13]

The attack in Central Park is just one of the many violent incidents that make the headlines. Two boys in Denver who were charged with stabbing a man for his credit cards so that they could buy camping equipment made the news. Numerous reports of incidents recounting teens killing teens for their jackets and other pieces of popular clothing are lumped together in one article. Beatings on city streets and in subways, the trashing of stores, and the killing of shopkeepers continue to occur without much notice by the general public. Even though violent incidents are reported daily, most do not reach the media in large cities.

Social agencies are concerned with the huge numbers of violent acts. Even though people's awareness of domestic violence has increased, no one knows exactly how much violence takes place in homes across the country. But as problems become more visible, researchers from many fields are exploring the subject: Why is there so much violence to and by today's young people? Why do some individuals act out their fantasies while others do not? In today's culture of violence, is wilding a tragic way of proving one's masculinity?

What has affected the minds of the young? Why are so many children growing up without feelings of mercy or compassion? These are questions that have been asked for many years, but they are asked more frequently today as teen mischief grows brutal.

A PUBLIC HEALTH PROBLEM

The development of the violent mind is complex, and the search for firm answers to questions about its causes is difficult. Many of the theories remain controversial, but they provide a base for exploration and a hope for prevention. Today scientists are trying to analyze violence in much the way they search for causes of and ways to prevent diseases like chicken pox and AIDS.

Researchers at the National Center for Health Statistics have recently reported that the homicide rate among young men in the United States is four to seventy-three times the rate in other industrial nations. The bar graph on page 23 compares the U.S. homicide rate with that of some selected countries. Experts point to a number of factors to explain the high level of vio-

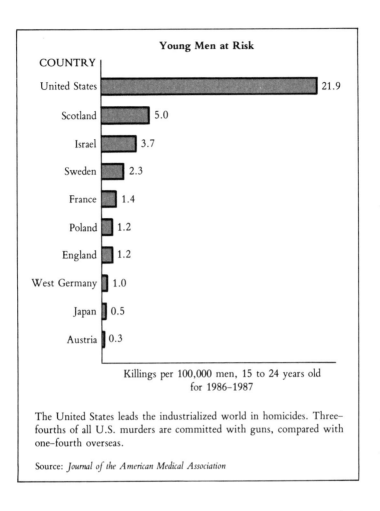

Young Men at Risk

COUNTRY

Country	Value
United States	21.9
Scotland	5.0
Israel	3.7
Sweden	2.3
France	1.4
Poland	1.2
England	1.2
West Germany	1.0
Japan	0.5
Austria	0.3

Killings per 100,000 men, 15 to 24 years old
for 1986–1987

The United States leads the industrialized world in homicides. Three-fourths of all U.S. murders are committed with guns, compared with one-fourth overseas.

Source: *Journal of the American Medical Association*

lence in America. The availability of firearms, which are used in three-fourths of the killings in this country, is considered to be a leading factor. Another is the drug epidemic. Homicide statistics began to climb as crack appeared on the streets. Violence in families and television violence are also cited as reasons for the high homicide rate in America.[14]

More girls are involved in violent crimes than in the past, in the country as well as in the city, probably because of their use of drugs; and relatively few of them have been sheltered from the violence around them. Researchers are asking whether or not girls get away with violent crime more easily than boys. They want to know why they are becoming more violent. One girl reported that she felt in control after she pulled the trigger to shoot her victim. A fourteen-year-old girl and her fifteen-year-old female friend stabbed an eighty-year-old woman twenty-eight times. Some girls have reported that killing gave them such a high that they wanted to do more.[15]

The magnitude and the tragedy of today's violence by and to the young cry out for more insights into its causes and new approaches in prevention and treatment. Large numbers of people live in fear of street violence today, but we know that violence is not new. The young are overrepresented in the world of violence, both as perpetrators and as victims. Young men are at higher risk of being murdered in the United States than in most other countries, and black men are especially vulnerable.[16] As violence against women has increased, the number of women who commit violence also has increased.

Brain damage and neurological diseases, peer pressure, domestic violence, poverty, and drugs all play a part in the violence committed in cities and rural areas. The violent mind has become a major public health problem, a political problem, and a deeply disturbing national crisis.

2
PROBING THE
BIOLOGICAL ROOTS
OF VIOLENCE

Are people born violent? Is aggression truly a fighting instinct in humans and animals that is directed against members of the same species? Is there something innate in humans that contributes to their violence?

BRAIN STRUCTURE AND VIOLENCE

The connection between biology and violence is a highly disputed subject. Scientists who study the anatomy of the human brain (see diagram, The Human Brain, on page 26) point out that the mechanism that *initiates* violence is located in an expansion of the brain stem, a tube of nervous tissue that connects the large part of the human brain to the spinal cord. This primitive part of the brain is similar to the kind of brain shared by prehistoric reptiles as well as turtles, alligators, and lizards. It is known in humans as the reptilian brain, or R complex.[1] It houses the mechanisms that control heartbeat, breathing, and sleep or wakefulness.[2]

The biological mechanisms for *controlling* violence are situated in a part located at the top of the brain stem. Known as the

EXTERIOR SURFACE OF THE LEFT BRAIN

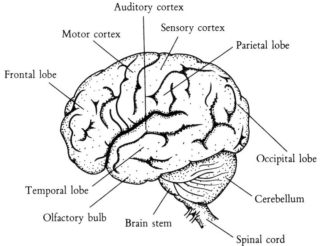

Auditory cortex

Motor cortex

Sensory cortex

Parietal lobe

Frontal lobe

Occipital lobe

Temporal lobe

Cerebellum

Olfactory bulb

Brain stem

Spinal cord

INTERIOR OF THE RIGHT BRAIN

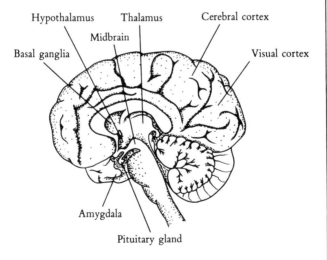

Hypothalamus   Thalamus   Cerebral cortex

Midbrain

Basal ganglia

Visual cortex

Amygdala

Pituitary gland

The Human Brain

Source: Ronald H. Bailey, *The Role of the Brain*, New York: Time–Life Books, 1975.

limbic brain, or limbic system, this part is sometimes called the "feeling" brain. If a part of a person's limbic system is damaged, sudden gusts of rage may sweep over the person.[3]

Evidence of the effect of damage to the limbic system is illustrated by the reactions of a person to rabies, a disease caused by a virus that infects the spinal cord and limbic brain. The word *rabies* literally means "rage," and it refers to the agitated, aggressive, and sometimes violent or bizarre behavior of a person whose limbic system has been invaded by the virus. Fortunately, inoculations can prevent this limbic damage, which, in the past, was almost always fatal.[4]

Although the systems that initiate and control violence are much the same in humans as in reptiles, rats, rabbits, kangaroos, and other animals, the human limbic system is governed by another part of the brain: the neocortex, or mammalian, brain. (A diagram illustrating the three main parts of the brain is provided on page 28.) People have elaborate systems of behavior beyond the basic "fight or flight" pattern of lower animals, giving them the ability to identify with the problems of others (empathy), to plan for the needs of others as well as themselves (logic), and to use knowledge to alleviate suffering (creativity).

An accident that occurred in the nineteenth century gave us clues to the connections between the deep emotional centers of the brain and the front part of the brain, or frontal lobes. Phineas Gage, a railway worker, suffered brain damage when an inch-thick (2.5 cm) iron rod was blasted through his head. Before the accident, this man was mild, steady, and efficient. After the accident, he was foul-mouthed and fitful. His personality changed so much that people said he was "no longer Gage." Doctors explained the fact that he was no longer himself by saying that the hole in his brain had caused an imbalance between his intellectual functioning and his "animal propensities."[5]

OLD THEORIES

In their search for the roots of human violence, people have suggested and believed in a wide variety of causes, including demons, witches, and the position of the stars. In the nineteenth

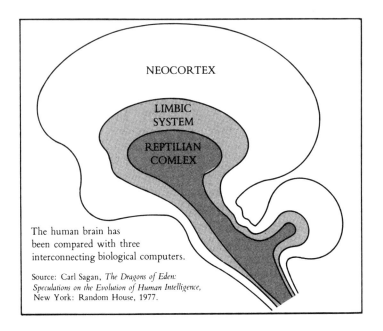

NEOCORTEX

LIMBIC
SYSTEM

REPTILIAN
COMLEX

The human brain has
been compared with three
interconnecting biological computers.

Source: Carl Sagan, *The Dragons of Eden:
Speculations on the Evolution of Human Intelligence,*
New York: Random House, 1977.

century, an Italian physician, Cesare Lombroso, introduced a theory of crime based on a person's physical characteristics. He examined many prisoners before and after their deaths, and he came to the conclusion that some people were "born criminal." He believed that physical traits such as a sloping forehead, long arms, and primitive brains were common among criminals. Lombroso and his colleagues considered criminals to be victims of bad biology as well as bad society.

Lombroso's methods and measurements were found to be flawed, and his "born criminal" theory did not survive. However, many studies were made by others to try to implicate physical characteristics as a cause of violence. For example, a number of criminologists tried to connect facial features with crime, but they did not succeed. Some searched extensively for the roots of crime and violence by comparing the body builds of delinquents and nondelinquents, but there was no serious evidence of a connection. However, James Q. Wilson does find the average offender to be constitutionally distinctive, although not extremely or abnormally so.[6]

The possibility of an extra chromosome—one of the

threadlike materials in cells that carry the genes, or blueprint of the body—was once thought to be involved in making minds violent. Normal females have a pair of X chromosomes (XX), and males have an X and a Y chromosome (XY) in all of their body cells. About one boy in a thousand is born with cells containing an extra male chromosome (XYY). As recently as the 1960s, some psychologists believed that this extra male chromosome predisposed these males, so-called supermales, to violence. They tend to be taller than average. (The police tend to single out tall men when they are called to break up a fight.)[7]

The chromosome theory of violence was popular about the time Richard Speck brutally killed eight nurses in Chicago in the summer of 1966. He knocked on the door of their dormitory and entered holding a knife. Later he produced a gun and held the nurses captive while he used strips of torn bedsheets to bind their hands behind their backs. Then he led them, one by one, to other rooms, where he murdered them. A ninth student nurse, who hid under a bed, lived to tell the horrible tale.[8]

At first, it was believed that Richard Speck had the XYY chromosome abnormality, and this tended to give credence to the chromosome theory of violence. However, it was later discovered that Speck actually did not have the extra Y chromosome. Further studies indicated that this chromosome abnormality had little to do with violence and other criminal activity. In fact, careful statistical work showed that 96 percent of men who have XYY chromosomes do not commit violent crimes.[9]

THE EPILEPSY MYTH

The myth that there is a strong connection between epilepsy and violence has been partially responsible for the stigma associated with the disease. Witnessing a seizure for the first time can be a frightening experience, and this may account for the false association of epilepsy and the violent mind. During a seizure, a person loses consciousness, and the limbs become rigid, the legs outstretched, and the arms bent. The limbs relax and then become rigid again, with gradually increasing intervals between spasms. Many other symptoms may be present when these convulsions occur.

Doctors describe a cause of the epileptic seizure as a firing of neurons that gets out of control, and, in most cases, this can be prevented by medication. Some forms of epilepsy cause an altered state of consciousness, during which an individual may exhibit strange behavior not under conscious control. But rarely is violence a symptom of an epileptic seizure.[10] Organized violent behavior has not been observed during epileptic seizures. Epilepsy is never the cause of premeditated crimes.

AGGRESSION AND ELECTRICAL BRAIN STIMULATION

Scientists have discovered some physical mechanisms in the brain that can result in aggression. One of the pioneers in implanting electrodes in the brain, Dr. Jose M. R. Delgado, experimented extensively with the relationship of electrical brain stimulation (EBS) and violence. In this procedure, a shaft was inserted through a small opening in the skull, and wires made of biologically inert materials were placed inside the brain. The upper portion of the shaft was bent over, and glued to, the bone surface, and a socket at the end was connected to sophisticated electronic technology. Hair wigs covered the stimulators, which can be controlled by a special radio apparatus. Many patients have said that they did not feel any discomfort from the presence of conductors in their heads even though they remained there for years.[11] Nonetheless, newer methods of experimentation rely less on the use of human subjects.

Delgado's most famous experiment involved the taming of a violent brain in a bull. After the bull was prepared with electrodes that could be controlled by radio stimulation, Delgado stepped into the bull ring. The fighting-mad bull bore down on him, but when the animal came near, Delgado stopped him by pressing a button on the portable stimulator. The bull skidded to a halt and began walking in circles.[12]

Although some people believe that the bull's violence was calmed by the electric stimulation in an "aggression center," many scientists think the stimulation caused the bull to turn its head, and this confused him. He may have become slightly disoriented rather than less aggressive. The idea of an "aggression center" is rejected today in light of new evidence showing that brain function involves many parts working in harmony.

Both before and after Delgado's famous experiment with the bull, many researchers explored the effects of EBS in a variety of animals. Cats were popular subjects for experiments. As far back as 1892, the role of the cortex was shown to be an inhibitor of violence. When the cortex was removed, animals lapsed into attacks of rage.[13] One man, Dr. Walter Rudolph Hess of Switzerland, mapped thousands of responses in experiments with 480 cats.[14]

Much of Dr. Hess's work involved the hypothalamus, a part of the brain that is below and tightly interconnected with the limbic system. Among other things, the hypothalamus is a command center for a host of complex states, one of which is anger. Electrical stimulation of one part of the hypothalamus can cause a cat to hiss, arch its back, and attack. Scientists call this kind of reaction "sham rage" because the cat is not really angry. In sham warfare, humans go through the rituals of aggression while observing regulations that limit their injuries. Football players appear to attack each other, but their actions are part of the sport. The rage response from electrical stimulation occurs without any provocation, and it disappears as quickly as it came. "Sham rage" can occur in humans whose violence is attributed to tumors in certain parts of the brain.[15]

The 1950s were a time of numerous experiments with laboratory animals to study their reactions after electrical stimulation to various parts of their brains. Through the years that followed, EBS was used to try to control problems in human patients, as in the famous case of Robert Parker.

In 1976, Parker was wired in an effort to tame his violent personality. He had been hospitalized since the age of thirteen and had spent most of his time in a ward for the severely disturbed or in a locked room under physical restraint. This man had nearly killed his sister, often slashed his wrists, and remained explosively violent in spite of doses of tranquilizers. After electrodes were implanted in Parker's brain, his violence ceased; according to reports, he was able to live outside the hospital.[16]

Robert Parker's violence may well have had a physical basis. Most mentally ill persons are not violent, but some exhibit bizarre behavior as a result of organic brain dysfunction.

Even when violence is just occasional, biologists believe that human minds are subject to many different control mechanisms that prevent the acting out of violent feelings. Few researchers deny that more crimes are committed by males than by females, but is the tendency to violence an inborn male trait? Although it is still less than the amount of male violence, female violent crime has increased in recent years. Is this due to a change in the place of women in society?

IS VIOLENCE INSTINCTIVE?

In their popular and widely read books on animals and human nature, Robert Ardrey and Konrad Lorenz argue that all humans are aggressive creatures by instinct.[17] In the 1960s, they proposed that it is this innate inclination toward violence that accounts for individual and group aggression.

According to Montagu, commenting on Lorenz's work, most vertebrates fight their own kind for sex, territory, and/or dominance. The strongest male gets the most desirable female, helping to assure that future generations inherit the stronger, more adaptive features. In addition, animals fight for their territory so that they have sufficient space in which to ensure an ample food supply. Most carnivorous, or meat-eating, animals, for example, appear to have definite territories from which strangers are excluded. Within the hunting territory of a wolf pack, strange wolves are attacked on sight. Many birds tend to have territories, and some sing territorial songs.

Humans tend to partition other people into friends or aliens. They tend to fear the actions of strangers and to solve conflict by aggression. Dominance, or pecking order, is found among wild and domestic animals as well as in humans. Social dominance is a sort of "law of the jungle" in which the stronger subdue the weaker.

The views of Robert Ardrey and his colleagues gave their readers a simple and welcome explanation for violence in humans, something people had been seeking for many years. These authors relied heavily on observations of animal behavior in drawing their conclusions. Lorenz was a noted zoologist and ethologist (one who studies the innate behavior of animals), and his belief that aggression and violence is instinctive in animals, including humans, is now quite controversial. Ashley Montagu edited a critique on the views of writers who support the idea of "innate depravity."[18]

According to Lorenz, animals display a wide variety of aggressive behaviors, but they usually stop short of killing their own kind. For example, a male gorilla fights fiercely with another, but the fight usually ends before there is a fatality. The struggle is harmless and ceremonial, ending with the weaker animal giving some sign of appeasement, such as a cringing posture or rolling over as if to await a mortal blow. That blow is seldom delivered by the victor.

Lorenz suggests that aggressive instinct is the force or drive necessary for survival of the species and that such behavior patterns are inherited. Most species have inherited inhibitions against aggression in their own species. Weapons such as teeth, claws, nasal horns, and antlers would be very dangerous if turned against members of the same species, so most fighting among animals is ritualized into display, threat, submission, and appeasement.

Many kinds of animals do, in certain situations, kill members of their own species. At times, male gorillas even kill members of their own troop. Lizards, elephants, hippopotamuses, and rodents sometimes fight to the death. Humans, according to Lorenz, show an incredible lack of inhibition against killing each other.[19]

However, many experts today believe that animal aggression based on territory, mating, and dominance has little to do with aggression in humans. Human aggression and violence are much more complicated than that of lower animals. Biologists do believe there are aggressive elements in a variety of instinctive behaviors, but there is no substance whatsoever to the arguments that "man is an aggressive animal" and "you can't change human nature."[20]

SOCIOBIOLOGY

While some researchers who look for the roots of violence put emphasis on social circumstances that surrounded the offender

33

(factors such as broken families, ineffective schools, poverty, unemployment, racism, and antisocial gang membership were popular among the reasons given as the roots of crime by these sociologists), others continue to emphasize the role of the genes.

A new science called sociobiology came to public view in 1975 in a book by Edward O. Wilson, *Sociobiology: The New Synthesis*. This book takes the view that genes and environment act as parts of a single system, sometimes together and sometimes separately. Sociobiologists believe that the mind is "hard wired" before birth with a predisposed personality rather than one that is mainly influenced by family and society. According to this theory, criminal tendencies and undesirable aggression may be biologically inevitable.[21]

VIOLENCE AS AN INDIVIDUAL CHOICE

In *Crime and Human Nature,* a book by James Q. Wilson and Richard J. Herrstein published in 1985, a case is made that both biological and social factors play roles in violent criminal behavior. After surveying masses of research reports in the fields of criminology, biology, psychology, anthropology, and others, these distinguished social scientists presented the theory that crime results from individual choice. The average violent offender may have been born with certain traits that make that individual more likely to be influenced by a violent environment. In other words, social forces that can activate criminal behavior in one person will not affect another.

This does not mean that criminals are born, not made. Many individual factors, such as age, sex, and intelligence, play a role, and all of these factors appear to be more important than race. A very small fraction of young males commits a large fraction of all violent street crimes, and males of all ages commit 82 percent of homicides. Eighty percent of homicides occur between members of the same race.[22] Black-on-black murder is the leading cause of death among black males aged fifteen to forty-four and is the leading cause of death among black females in the fifteen-to-thirty-four age group. A black man has a 1 in 21 chance of becoming a homicide victim.[23] Most of this violence is attributed to poverty.

34

THE TRACE ELEMENT THEORY

Scientists who are probing for biological roots of crime today are looking for factors that can help its prevention. They search for linkages in hormonal levels and other areas of body chemistry, like the genetic factors that lead to alcohol addiction, to learn more about what creates a violent mind. Studies are complex and wide-ranging. For example, two criminologists, Dr. Paul Cromwell and Ben Abadie from the University of Texas, are searching for an explanation of violent behavior by new studies on the presence in the body of all sorts of metals and minerals, such as zinc, copper, magnesium, potassium, and iron.[24]

Human hair is a good guide to the concentration of metals and minerals in the whole body. It may indicate that they take part in reactions in the brain, and there is a growing body of research suggesting that minerals might influence behavior. In their research, Cromwell and Abadie took hair samples from prisoners who had records of violence and compared them with samples from nonviolent inmates. Through careful scientific analysis, they found a clear pattern. Violent criminals consistently had abnormal levels of at least one metal or mineral. Although such studies are valuable, more research must be done. If it is learned that such chemical differences play a part in the development of violent minds, this could help in both prevention and treatment.

Scientists have searched for the biological roots of violence in many more ways than are mentioned in this chapter, and they will continue to do so. Studies that stress the importance of nature over nurture, as well as those that indicate that nurture is more important, are numerous. Some personality studies find that traits are mostly inherited; others emphasize the role of learning in the development of personality. Today there is a strong trend toward acknowledging the roles of both genetic coding and cultural and environmental experiences. And there is an increasing realization that there is still much to learn about the causes of violence.

3
LEARNING TO
BE VIOLENT

Why has human life become so devalued for thousands of children? What have been their lessons in violence? Although violence is a tragic reality in the world of today's adolescents, the vast majority of young people grow up to contribute to their communities in many positive ways. Most violent minds mature into controlled behaviors; and although the glamour and appeal of violence remains, they are provided by books, television, and other media rather than by reality. Only a small percentage of young people commit most violent crimes, and even some of them outgrow their violent and destructive behavior.

LEARNING VIOLENCE ON THE STREET

Consider the case of Shawn. He is eighteen years old and has a history of youth violence and gang activity. He lives with his mother, stepfather, and younger sister and brother in a section of a large city where violence is common. The following excerpt appeared in a statement prepared for his appearance before the House Select Committee on Children, Youth and Families at a hearing in March 1988:

I am enrolled in the Day Treatment Program because I am involved in intensive probation as the result of committing a robbery. I committed the robbery because I am a member of the Cedar Avenue Gang. I have been a member for the past three years. We spend our time getting high by drinking beer, smoking marijuana, and using a little cocaine. When we are high we will do anything. . . . There are more than 100 gang members. The leader is a nineteen year old who has been a member since he was ten years old.

Like many of the other gang members, I grew up in a single parent household. My father has had little contact with me since I was one year old. In my neighborhood, a lot of negative things go on. People sell drugs, a lot of the gang members' parents use drugs, and often these guys do not see their parents. Mostly, guys do not talk about their families.

We usually get together at other guys' houses. We do not usually meet at my house because my mother has a lot of nice things and I think that some of the guys may steal something or break something.

When I was young, I used to wonder about my father. I also resented his not being in my life. Now I do not care. However, I think that I would not have become involved in a gang if I had had a job and if my father had had a relationship with me. . . .

When we get high, I am the gang member with the most mouth. I am also doing better than all the other members academically. They are either dropouts or they are behind in their grades. I am the only member who is in the twelfth grade. If I had not become a member of the gang I would be out of high school and attending college now. When I joined the gang I stopped going to school or I did poorly. When I was placed on intensive probation, I started attending school regularly and doing well in class. I must also observe curfew. The other gang members laugh at me. I hang with them when I can. I can't leave the gang because they . . . would probably hurt me for trying to leave. . . .

If we still live in the same neighborhood when my five year old brother comes of age, I plan to steer him away from the gang. I do not like being a member but I have no choice.[1]

LEARNING VIOLENCE AT HOME

Many young people involved in gang warfare continue to live with violence as a way of dealing with problems. They grew up learning violence from their peers and, in many cases, from their own families. Of the total instances of violent crime, violence in the home is considered most common.[2] Misty is one of the thousands of children whose lessons in violence began at home.

Thirteen-year-old Misty is a young mother who has left her six-month-old baby with her own mother and is living in a shelter for the homeless. Misty wants to go home, but she still has bruises on her back from the last beating her mother's boyfriend gave her. When she lived at home, Misty was often beaten with switches and belts because she did something wrong. Sometimes she was beaten because her brother said she did something wrong, even when she really had not. These beatings started years before her baby was born.

About two years ago, when Misty was eleven, her teacher noticed the welts on her arm the first day she went to school in a short-sleeved polo shirt. Misty usually wore long sleeves, even in hot weather, so that no one would see her bruises. The teacher insisted on taking Misty to the principal's office, where there was a discussion about how Misty was treated at home. Even though she hated her mother's lover, Misty refused to reveal who beat her. The school principal called the family service agency and asked them to investigate Misty's home situation. After finding cuts and bruises on her back, the social worker took pictures of them for the court proceedings. It was decided that Misty should be taken away from her family. After a short stay in the hospital for treatment, she went to a foster home.

Life with a foster family was better than life at home in some ways. No one beat her there, and it was fun to live with five other children about her own age, even though there was a great deal of fighting. Misty kept one of the younger girls under control by hitting her, and she was punished for this. Misty did have one special friend, a boy who always took her side in a fight. Misty loved him so much that she was happy to go along with anything he wanted to do. She enjoyed his hugs and kisses, and before long, the two were enjoying sex together. When she was twelve years old, Misty learned that she was pregnant.

The family service agency moved Misty back with her mother, who now had a new live-in lover. He was not pleased to have Misty around, and he let her know this by punishing her for every little thing that displeased him. The punishment usually took the form of a beating with his belt.

About three months after her baby was born, Misty decided to leave the baby with her mother and try life on the street. There she found more hunger, more sex, and more violence. No wonder she wants to go home to take care of her baby.

How do you think Misty will deal with the problems that come with raising a baby? Might she try to control the child with violence?

Although this is not always the case, violence learned at home can frequently extend from one generation to the next. Some parents who grew up in violent homes believe beatings are the only form of discipline that works. Abusers can be lawyers or doctors as well as factory workers and custodians. They live in the city, the country, and the suburbs. They can be drunks, cocaine addicts, or people who never use illegal drugs. Usually, abusers use violence to get something they want. A husband may want comfort from his wife but does not know how to ask for it. In blaming her for his problem, he may become violent because this is his way of controlling the situation.

However, violence learned in the home does not always

carry over from one generation to the next. There is a popular expression, "violence begets violence," but new studies indicate that only about one-third of those who were abused as children will grow up to abuse their own children. The majority, two-thirds, will not.[3] This does not mean that lessons in violence are not learned from both parents and friends. A shy, passive child who runs away from home soon learns that violence is a part of life on the street. It does mean that better ways of parenting can be taught to protect those children who would normally be at risk.

The argument about nature versus nurture is an old one. At one time, many people believed that a baby's mind is a blank slate on which environment writes the program. However, most scientists now believe that both heredity and environment play their roles in determining the behavior and life-style of an individual. How big a role each plays is a subject of controversy to this day.

DOMESTIC VIOLENCE

Even though much progress is being made in helping people to use words instead of physical force to solve their problems, domestic violence is still widespread. The increase in child abuse is causing great concern throughout the nation, but children are not the only family members who suffer abuse.

The abuse of elderly family members occurs far more often than most people realize, for it is difficult to believe that adults would strike their helpless parents. However, according to a survey by the House Select Committee on Aging, about 1.5 million elderly Americans are physically hurt or threatened by family members each year. The number may be even greater, for the social isolation of the elderly means abuse is likely to be undetected.[4]

Many abusers of the elderly feel powerless, and this makes them so angry and frustrated that they vent that anger on old people who depend on them. For example, Joe was guilty of elder abuse. His mother was confused, incontinent, blind, and uncooperative. She had to be dressed, washed, fed, cleaned when she soiled herself, and as if this were not enough, she would not cooperate in her care. When Joe tried to feed her, she refused to eat. When he managed to get food in her mouth, she would take the food out and hide it in her pocket. Caring for Joe's mother would have been a challenge for anyone, let alone a young working man with no help. The abuse of this woman rose out of the mental, physical, and emotional burdens of caring for her. Reporters who covered this case of elder abuse described Joe as a victim of circumstances.[5]

By 1990, twenty-seven states had installed elder abuse hot lines and 43 had laws that require police, health workers, and social workers to report cases of elder abuse.[6]

Although elder abuse is one example of domestic abuse, it is *younger women* who are the main victims. Estimates of the number of women battered by their husbands or partners range from 1 million to 3 million per year. An estimated 30% to 50% of murdered women are killed by their partners.[7] Crimes by spouses or ex-spouses make up 57 percent of all crimes committed by relatives.[8]

Wife battering has long been accepted in a wide variety of families. While smacking a neighbor would be considered assault, hitting a wife could seem like a family argument in which a man was asserting his right of control. Today this kind of behavior is no longer acceptable, but in many families, men continue to have traditional ideas about the relationship between husband and wife. They believe that what they do to their families in private does not really count. Home is the one place where they can express their violence without being punished for it.

Although what happens in the mind of each violent man is different, there is a pattern of three stages in many battering relationships. Katie's husband had a good job but did not pay the household bills. His main interest was cocaine, and this took up most of his money. Katie hated to hear a knock on the door, for she felt certain it would be a bill collector, a person to shut off the electricity, or someone bringing an eviction notice. Day after day, her husband insulted her, belittled her, badgered her, and threatened her. This tension-building stage could last for weeks or months before it built up to actual physical assault. This second stage, the explosive one in which the assault actually occurred, was followed by a third stage in which he said he was sorry, showered Katie with gifts, and promised never to hurt her again.

This kind of violence usually happens again and again until the woman escapes from the marriage or is fatally wounded, or the man is arrested and/or gets help from professionals. Many people wonder why battered wives put up with the violence. Some even say that they must like it. It is true that many wives feel that somehow they must deserve such treatment, but even if they want to leave, they are dependent on their husbands for support. Rather than ask why battered wives stay in such situations, people might ask where the battered wife can go if she leaves her home. How can she care for her children? What are her options?

The battering of women is so common that many states have passed mandatory arrest laws. As early as 1980, forty-eight states had passed some kind of domestic violence legislation, but the plight of women who still suffer from the violence that explodes when their partners use force to solve their problems is extensive. The number of groups offering counseling to male batterers has increased greatly within the last five years. However, there is only a 25 percent success rate with the men who attend the groups. Unfortunately, many batterers do not perceive themselves to be in need of help. Anne Menard of the Connecticut Coalition Against Domestic Violence has suggested a national campaign against violence toward women similar to the one against drinking and driving.[9]

While most spousal violence victimizes women, some violence occurs against husbands and ex-husbands. Spouses and lovers who batter each other, children and adults who batter their parents, parents who batter their children, friends and strangers who batter each other learned violence, in many cases, as a way of dealing with problems when they were very young children.

42

VIOLENCE AND THE MEDIA

In their search for the causes of violence, psychologists, sociologists, and criminologists propose a wide array of theories. A common denominator among these theories is the belief that violent individuals learn violence from watching it happen. As mentioned earlier, even though being maltreated as a child increases the chance that a person will be abusive as an adult, most battered children do not continue the cycle of violence that was once considered inevitable. But what about watching violence on television or in the community? Almost everyone sees a great deal of violence, either in real life or on the screen. In many cases, the violence is promoted as an effective way of dealing with human conflict.

Many experiments illustrate the effects of witnessing violence. One classic series of studies was done by Albert Bandura and his associates. The basic procedure was to have children watch an adult knock around a plastic air-filled Bobo doll (the kind that bounces back after it has been knocked down). In the experiment the children not only imitated the behavior of the adults, but they introduced new kinds of aggressive behavior.

According to Bandura, the results of the experiments leave little doubt that exposure to violence heightens aggressive tendencies in children. Although children who watch violence on television are not going to attack the first person they see, if they are provoked on some future occasion, they may well imitate the aggressive patterns of behavior they learned from watching television.[10]

Professor Leonard Eron studied the effect of television on children for many years. In 1960 he interviewed 875 third-graders. Ten years later, he interviewed 427 children from the same group, the ones he could locate. In 1981, he again was able to locate and interview 409 children from the original group. Professor Eron concluded from his studies that excessive viewing of violence on television causes increased aggression.[11]

Many individuals, including some psychologists, claim that violence on television does not trigger aggression. For example, psychologist Dr. Seymour Feshback studied the effects of television violence on two groups of semidelinquent youths and came to the conclusion that the group that watched boisterous adventure shows had a tendency to be less aggressive than the group that watched neutral shows.[12]

Some researchers, such as Professor Jib Fowles, argue that television violence can decrease hostile feelings by means of catharsis, the purging of repressed emotions. If people identify with certain characteristics and act out harbored emotions, such as fear and anger, vicariously through watching television, they discharge their own pent-up aggressions safely.[13] Violence used in the name of the law is approved by society, and children can identify with certain characteristics and vicariously act out their harbored emotions, according to those who defend violence in television.

Another argument for the benefits of violence in television claims that people feel more relaxed after watching a violent film on television. Still another points to the fact that Japanese television airs many shows that are full of violence and gore and the Japanese are among the least violent of all people. Could it be that exposure to violence on television is irrelevant to violence in the real world?

The relationship of media and violence will always be controversial. What may be true for one viewer will not be true for another, for each individual comes with a different biology and different experiences.

The role of television in a murder that was committed by Ronney Zamora at the age of fifteen was a major factor in his trial in 1977. It was a landmark case because an edited version of the trial, which was held in Miami, Florida, aired on national television. Ronney Zamora shot and killed an eighty-two-year-old widow who lived next door to him. She happened to walk into her house while Ronney and a friend were in the midst of burglarizing it. The boys took $400, and Ronney shot the woman in the stomach with a pistol he had found in her house.

The defense pleaded "involuntary television intoxication," stating that excessive exposure to television violence had distorted the boy's concept of right and wrong.[14] Although Ronney was convicted of the crime, many experts believe that exposure to television violence does incite violence in the real world. It tends to desensitize viewers and create the impression that we truly live in a mean and dangerous world.

Although "mean streets" exist in some communities, most people are not prone to violence. As Gilda Berger concludes in *Violence and the Media,* "the principal message we . . . get from the media is that violence is an exciting, sometimes rewarding, and necessary part of life."[15]

VIOLENCE IN SPORTS

Television and violence are connected in interactive games, too. Playing violent games is nothing new for boys, but days that include four hours of action-packed television and some video games that encourage a player to punch, shoot, and destroy by means of a joystick may have serious effects on young minds. In addition to being robbed of time for creative play, viewers and video game players can lose touch with the consequences of violence.

Participants in sports can learn to be violent and aggressive in the pressure to win. Against a backdrop of rapidly escalating violence in everyday life, there seems to be an increasing amount of violence in the world of sports. Many children are getting the message "win at any cost." The amount of violence in competitive sports is seen in both players and spectators. For many professional players, violence is the name of the game. Violent incidents during games and among spectators are highlighted by the media, and it may be that people are becoming so desensitized to violence in sports that they seek more of it. As noted, the theory that aggression is relieved by watching violent action on television has been almost completely rejected by researchers in the field. Sports can be fun without violence, a point that needs to be taught early in the lives of boys and girls.[16]

While everyone becomes angry at times, most people learn to manage their own angry and aggressive outbursts. When examples of acceptable ways of coping are learned from parents, in school, or in other areas of the environment, violent actions are viewed as inappropriate. But many children grow up in an atmosphere of violence at home and on the streets. And they come to believe, from watching television and sports, that violence pays off.

No matter where one learns to be violent, it is generally agreed that human nature can be changed. Although there seem to be some exceptions, most violent minds can be tamed.

4
DRUGS AND THE VIOLENT MIND

Headline after headline proclaims the connection between violence and drugs: "Four Slayings Called Drug Related," "Addict Guilty in Crack Rampage Killing," "Suspect in Killing Tests Positive for Crack and PCP." You could make a long list of drug-related crimes by combing just a few months' coverage in large city newspapers. However, the relationship between drugs and crime can vary. That there *is* a relationship between the two has once even been a matter of dispute.

"Everyone knows that drugs make people violent" is a common statement, but it is not totally true. Some drugs make people more violent; others make them less so. Even in the case of crack, the drug most often associated with violence, there is some controversy about how much direct effect there is.[1]

THE LINK BETWEEN DRUGS AND CRIME

Drugs and violence are related in several ways. Drug dealers' fighting over turf is described in Chapter 5. Some kinds of drugs make individuals act in violent ways, often because of addiction

47

and the need for money to buy drugs to prevent withdrawal or to satisfy one's craving. A heroin addict may feel mellow and sleepy until withdrawal makes him or her willing to mug someone for money for the next fix. Although the violence that takes place here is drug-related, heroin intoxication itself does not cause it. The user actually becomes passive under the influence of this drug. Some addicts may even be medicating themselves to suppress aggressive feelings.[2]

Individuals who are violent under the influence of alcohol and possibly other drugs are also violent, or have violent tendencies, when not involved with drugs. Violence depends on many factors, and in any one incident situational, biological, cultural, genetic, and social factors may be intermingled. Whether violence or drug abuse comes first is often debated, but there is much evidence that criminal activity frequently begins before the involvement with drugs. After that, drugs and crime reinforce one another.[3] The debate over whether drug use causes crime or crime causes drug use continues, but it is now beyond question that the two are related. When drug users are in a period of active use, rates of criminality go up dramatically. And conversely, during periods of abstinence, rates of criminality go down.[4]

ALCOHOL AND DRUGS

The graph on page 49 shows that, while drug use has declined for eighteen-year-olds, drinking alcohol has not.

There is more support for the direct effect of alcohol on violence than for many illicit drugs.[5] Although many people who drink alcohol to excess do not become violent, alcohol is a significant factor in the three leading causes of death for young people: accidents, homicide, and suicide.[6] In the case of suicide, alcohol is seldom believed to be the main cause of self-inflicted violence. Many of the injuries and about half of the deaths in automobile accidents are alcohol-related. Drunken pilots, bus drivers, and train operators add to the list. Alcohol has long been associated with a wide variety of other crimes, too, including wife beating, child abuse, rape, and sexual crimes committed against children.

48

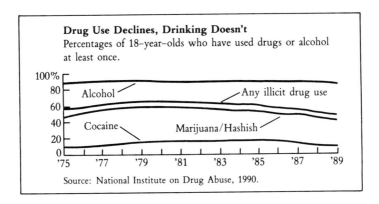

Drug Use Declines, Drinking Doesn't
Percentages of 18-year-olds who have used drugs or alcohol at least once.

Source: National Institute on Drug Abuse, 1990.

Alcohol alters the brain's chemistry. By weakening a person's inhibitions, in some cases, it sets in motion a considerable amount of violent behavior. A number of theories has been advanced to explain the effects of alcohol on aggression. One theory suggests that alcohol adversely affects the nervous system and that this reduces one's conscious control over one's behavior. Others suggest that the effects of alcohol on the central nervous system are more direct. Alcohol use reduces the capacity to process information and results in a tendency to attend to only the most obvious cues in the environment.[7]

Small amounts of alcohol do not incite users to violence, and excessive amounts make violent behavior impossible. But violence can, and frequently does, emerge with moderate to large amounts. Almost everyone knows a person, normally very mild, who becomes aggressive after drinking.

The story of Jeff is the case of a man whose personality seemed to change completely after he became drunk. Normally, he depended on his wife for support because he felt worthless and inadequate. A first drink always led to many, so he usually did not drink at home. But in the evenings, he went to the local bar, where he and his friends "tied one on." He felt secure with his friends, who also drank excessively.

One evening when Jeff was having a pleasant meal with his family, they began talking about his parents. He had grown up

49

far from his current home, his parents had died before he was married, and his wife and children often wished they knew more about that part of their family. Jeff wanted to forget his childhood, for it was one that was filled with fighting and violence. By confining his drinking to the local bar, Jeff was able to keep the promise he made to himself that his own children would have a peaceful home. However, the questions about his childhood brought tears to his eyes. He went into the bedroom and stayed there for a long time. While in the bedroom, Jeff broke open a bottle of vodka that he had hidden in his drawer, and when he came out, he was very drunk. He was also very violent.

Jeff's family knew that he was very different when he came home from evenings at the bar, but they were not prepared for the scene that followed. He hit his wife until she was unconscious, then he beat the children. When the effects of the alcohol wore off, Jeff was very upset about what he had done. He promised not to hurt his family again, but he no longer kept his rule of not drinking at home. The battering grew more frequent, and his promises to change were never kept.

The abuse of alcohol appears to be common among wife beaters. This violence may serve to release the husband momentarily from his anxiety about his ineffectiveness as a man.[8] Feelings of bravado or omnipotence while drunk can wipe out one's sense of caution and prudence, and one can become dangerous to oneself and others.

PCP AND VIOLENCE

PCP (phencyclidine) is an illegal drug that was once called the peace pill, but it frequently produces symptoms that are the opposite of peaceful. PCP is sometimes called rocket fuel and killer weed, names that seem more fitting than its common name, angel dust. Users of PCP can have delusions of power along with insensitivity to pain, and this combination can lead to strange and extreme forms of violence. This commonly used drug is one of the most dangerous.[9]

Police encounters with PCP-intoxicated individuals are

50

associated frequently with violent, assaultive, combative, suicidal, and even homicidal behavior. Even the shining of a flashlight in a suspect's eyes may trigger aggressive action. Users may be ambivalent and unpredictable, even toward their close friends and relatives. PCP affects the mind in a way that makes one element (often violent in nature) of the user's personality dominant.

Frequently, PCP users consider themselves endowed with unique and superior abilities. Since users may feel no pain, they may injure themselves as well as the people they attack. Bystanders have often been furiously attacked because users are paranoid, living in an unreal world in which they believe people are out to persecute them. Many users tend to repeat the same violent acts. No one knows how many crimes have been committed because of PCP, for many users have histories of violent behavior.[10]

PCP has been known to cause flashbacks in the weeks or months after the effects seem to have worn off. During these flashbacks, users can suddenly feel threatened and lash out at the supposed threat with the same amount of violence fueled by their feelings of omnipotence when they took the drug.

AMPHETAMINES AND VIOLENCE

Ice, crank, meth, speed, glass, and other forms of drugs classified as amphetamines are reported to be linked with acts of senseless violence. These stimulants can produce long-lasting rage reactions and irrational suspicion that leads to violence. There may be a tendency to repeat acts for long periods of time. Cases of continual stabbing or clubbing of a victim after death are known to be associated with the use of amphetamines, especially when combined with PCP.

Consider the case of Mark, known to his friends as a speed freak. Mark would inject speed as often as ten times a day, getting an intense feeling of pleasure each time. Between injections, Mark felt "high," and he was very excitable and active. After two or three days, Mark was exhausted from lack of food

51

and sleep, and he would crash (sleep for 24 to 48 hours). When he awakened, he would eat a tremendous amount of food. Then came the depression and the search for more speed to begin another binge. One time his binge was followed by deep depression, along with terrifying hallucinations in which he mistook friends for wild animals. He lashed out with murderous rage at both real and imagined intrusions to his surroundings. At this point, Mark's friends took him to the emergency room of the local hospital so that he would not seriously harm himself or someone else.

THE MARIJUANA STORY

During the 1930s, many people believed that marijuana use was responsible for considerable violence. The Commissioner of Narcotics, Henry J. Anslinger, led a campaign against marijuana by using scare tactics. He lent his name to atrocity stories, and in one tale "an entire family was murdered by a youthful (marijuana) addict in Florida. When officers arrived at the home they found the youth staggering around in a human slaughterhouse."[11] Many such stories were part of a campaign to discourage the use of this "demon drug" as a gateway to violence.

The term "dope fiend" was commonly used to describe a user, but those who smoked marijuana learned that it had a calming effect. They quickly dismissed these accounts about marijuana as propaganda. As a result, many drug users tended not to believe true statements that warned of the ill effects of other drugs.

STEROIDS AND VIOLENCE

Many athletes use steroids to try to gain an advantage in strength, stamina, and speed in competitions. One of the side effects of the use of these drugs can be violence. In a recent report, the use of steroids was blamed for its role in the violent crimes of three weight lifters who had been using multiple steroids. In one case, a woman made a remark that was meant to be humorous, but it upset the weight lifter so much that he kidnapped her and shot her when she tried to escape. She is now a paraplegic. In the second case, a hitchhiker was tied between two poles and killed by the weight lifter, who kicked him and beat him with a piece of wood. The third weight lifter, apparently on the suggestion and with the assistance of an acquaintance, tried, unsuccessfully, to blow up the car of his ex-fiancée.

After the effect of the steroids wore off, all three men expressed extreme remorse and suffered from depression. Psychiatrists learned that the men had been mild-mannered before their use of steroids and that they had not exhibited violent behavior before using the drugs. One of the men had an identical twin, who was also a weight lifter, but he had not shown signs of violent behavior. Investigators suggest that the steroid use was the only differentiating factor between the two brothers. They also believe that steroids may have contributed to other violent crimes that have not been documented.[12]

COCAINE AND VIOLENCE

Cocaine and the smokable form of cocaine called crack can affect minds in such a way that violent behavior results. Although much of the cocaine-related violence that has been blamed for the homicide epidemic stems from wars among drug dealers over turf, some of it is reported to be the result of the medical and biological effects of cocaine itself.

Four stages have been identified as aftereffects of the use of cocaine. In the first stage, feelings of euphoria may be accompanied by insomnia, hyperactivity, and a tendency toward violence. When the level of cocaine in the blood starts to fall, then apathy, sadness, anxiety, and aggressiveness set in. These feelings increase as time goes on, and they are accompanied by an irresistible craving to use more cocaine.

With more cocaine, users can progress to a stage called cocaine hallucinosis, in which there are paranoid thoughts such as "the police are out to get me," as well as hallucinations and distortions of known objects in the environment. Although users in this stage are aware that their perceptions are not correct, they often arm themselves with weapons for use in the next and final stage, known medically as cocaine psychosis. Emotional problems are exaggerated, and if enough of the drug is ingested, cocaine can induce loss of reality even among healthy individuals. In cocaine psychosis, abusers are convinced that their hallucinations and delusions are real, and they may actually harm those they perceive to be threatening them.[13] Smokers who wrongfully accuse each other of stealing crack sometimes attack each other with knives or with the butane torches used to smoke the drug.

Consider the case of B. W., as described by Dr. J. Reid Meloy. After using cocaine for an entire night, B. W. thought he saw two men lurking outside. He sent his girl friend and her daughter away so that they would be safe. After they left, B. W. was alone in the apartment, but he sensed that the window shades were moving and the closet door in the bedroom was sliding. He was sure that there were men hiding in the closet who were going to kill him. Then he began to feel dizzy, thinking that someone had turned on the gas outside his apartment. To protect himself from the gas, B. W. took a chair and began smashing windows. Then he believed he saw the front door move. Now he felt that attack was imminent, and he began to pace back and forth and break more windows to get the attention of others. He heard voices that told him there was no way out, so he should make a run for it. He tried to fire his gun, but it jammed, and he believed this was further evidence that he was being framed.

When B. W. realized he had cut himself on the window glass and was bleeding profusely, he tied a tourniquet on his arm and went into the bathroom. He barricaded himself there, thinking that was the only way he could protect himself. He fired his gun into the air several times. The SWAT team, who arrived after gunshots were heard, threw tear gas inside and entered the apartment. B. W. was shot in the crossfire, but he recovered and was able to describe his feelings in detail to the doctors who evaluated his condition.

B. W. made it clear that he did not recognize the SWAT

team as the police. He had believed that the "men hiding in the closet" had made a getaway and had escaped detection of the SWAT team. Although the SWAT team was certain that they were being attacked by B.W., B.W. believed that he was defending himself against a gang of drug dealers.

The doctors who examined B.W. after the incident all came to the conclusion that he was suffering from "cocaine delusional disorder" at the time of the offense. His violence was typical of the kind experienced by many long-term cocaine users, except that it was made more intense by his paranoid personality.[14]

The agitation caused by paranoia and psychosis can make it difficult to get a disturbed cocaine user to a hospital. The agitation can also make it difficult to get someone who has overdosed to a hospital. (Cocaine overdose can cause heart failure, stroke, seizures, coma, and respiratory collapse. A binge may result in sudden death.) Police are advised to handle these people gingerly, using handcuffs to restrain those who are difficult to manage. Even with their hands cuffed behind their backs, some of them still kick and thrash so violently that they hurt themselves.

MULTIPLE DRUG USE

One of the problems in studying the relationship of illegal drugs and violent minds is the fact that there is no way to control these studies. There is not even a reliable estimate of the number of people who combine different kinds of drugs, but new studies of criminal suspects indicate that large numbers of users are involved in polydrug use. In Washington, D.C., the Pretrial Services Agency conducts a five-drug screen of arrestees. They are tested for PCP (angel dust), cocaine, opiates (heroin, opium, morphine), methadone (a drug used in heroin treatment programs), and amphetamines (speed, meth, ice, crank, glass, etc.). When the program was begun in 1984, slightly over half of all arrestees tested positive for more than one drug. In 1988, the figure was three out of four, and the trend continues upward.[15]

Eric D. Wish, a visiting fellow at the National Institute of

Justice, estimated there may be as many as 1.3 million regular cocaine users among criminal suspects in major metropolitan areas. This means that the number of hard-core cocaine addicts may be far greater than original estimates since the criminals were not counted in regular government surveys.[16] No one knows how many of these people may have suffered overdoses and/or have become violent.

Family court judges believe that crack has produced an epidemic involving children being beaten, raped, and murdered by their own families. Many grandparents assume care of children born to drug-abusing mothers. Although these substitute parents may desperately need help with health care and food costs, they are frequently reluctant to apply for it because such action can lead to confrontation with the addicted parent, who is often ill and violent.

THE TRAGEDY OF CRACK BABIES

Mothers addicted to cocaine are more apt to neglect their children than to treat them violently, but many of these children suffer from both neglect and physical abuse. The number of child abuse cases has been rising along with the number of substance-abusing mothers. Many child abuse specialists believe that not enough is being done to learn more about the problems of children of cocaine abusers.

Children whose parents use crack report being slapped and beaten, but infants cannot tell of the violence inflicted on them. In at least two cases of infant death, medical examiners believe that crack must have been administered directly into the infants' bloodstream.

Cocaine and other drugs also affect children before birth. There is little doubt that thousands of crack babies suffer from damaged nervous systems. Just a single hit of cocaine before a woman discovers she is pregnant can affect the fetus.[17] A diminished blood supply may result in a smaller-than-normal head size and low birth weight. One crack baby was described as having arms and legs the size of matchsticks. Crack babies who survive to school age are likely to go through life with damaged brains. Crack affects the newly born in a number of different and tragic ways. In addition to running the risk of a stroke just before or after birth, crack babies tend to go from sleeping to screaming. Such babies have little chance of normal bonding with their mothers and of early learning—both important factors in the development of a healthy child. Crack babies cannot be cuddled like normal babies, for they tend to be very stiff. At the age of four months, they may even be rigid, and they have trouble bringing their hands together and relaxing their fists.[18] These babies suffer from stomach cramps, do not fall into normal sleep patterns, and may suffer from seizures. Some cry incessantly, one of the signs that the baby's nervous system is overloaded.

For a mother trying to remain drug-free, having a baby who screams inconsolably at the slightest provocation can provoke violent abuse. Even the healthiest mother can have a hard time helping a baby who starts to cry when she looks at it. Some mothers of crack babies are in treatment programs, learning how to stimulate their babies without overstimulating them. These mothers learn the signs of overstimulation and are shown how to swaddle the babies in blankets to help calm them. But such programs are scarce.

Many crack babies are lethargic; they have trouble developing motor skills and relating to people. Like all babies, they eat and sleep, eat and sleep again and again, but they seem to tune out the world. As they grow older, crack babies seem unable to play creatively. While children of the same age level play with their toys, crack babies tend to bat at toys, throw them across the room, or pick them up and put them down without purpose.[19]

Crack babies continue to have problems as they grow older. One teacher says that they seem to operate only on an instinctual level, and that they have difficulty learning. No one knows how to undo the damage caused by the cocaine that ravaged them before they were born.[20]

No one knows the full extent of violence that can be

traced to the use of drugs by pregnant women. Crack babies have yet to grow into adults, but the predictions for their future are not good. A number of these babies are never claimed and may spend a year in a nursery, with all sorts of psychological ramifications.[21] No one knows how many of these babies will grow into children who will express their frustrations through violence.

Violence committed by those who use drugs and by the children of drug users is a serious health problem. In addition to the violence caused by the drug users themselves, there is considerable violence on the part of dealers, who fight for customers. By 1991, six years after the beginning of the crack epidemic, many young people are resisting the drug because they see the damage it has inflicted on their parents and siblings. But crack is still sold openly, and some experts believe that while many young people are turning to other drugs, the fight for a shrinking crack market has increased the number of shootouts and murders. No matter what the trend, violence and drugs remain related. Far more help is needed from professionals and volunteers in preschool and school programs to prevent drug abuse and to help those who do not use drugs but live in a drug-related climate of violence.

5
DOWN THESE MEAN
STREETS

Violent crimes throughout America are committed by a dispro-
portionately small number of individuals, the vast majority of
whom live on "these mean streets."[1] Whole neighborhoods are
riddled with poverty, and hopes have been shattered by lack of
medical care, poor schools, and few opportunities for jobs. In
Watts, a ghetto section of Los Angeles, a health worker asked a
group of school children to tell her what they considered was
the most important thing in their lives. Many of them told her it
was staying alive. She remarked that they responded as though
they were at war.[2]

VIOLENCE WITHOUT GUILT

Violence by and against children in America has shocked and
outraged the nation. Much of the violence seems senseless; fighting over a pair of sneakers can lead to murder. There are children who have killed without seeming to feel much remorse,
acting as if murder is something that just happens.

A twelve-year-old who shot a stockbroker in Corpus
Christi, Texas, blew the smoke out of the barrel of his gun, then

got on his bike and rode away. After a young man shot and killed a store clerk, he was asked if he had "respect for life." He answered affirmatively and added that he had killed only one other person before he killed the store clerk.

In poor sections of American cities, an increasing number of young people are killing for clothes that they feel will help them emulate sports figures. And some killings are carried out by gangs who see people wearing a color that makes them think the wearer belongs to a rival gang. Sometimes the victim is unaware that the color is favored by any gang. One little girl in a red sweater died after she was hit over the head with a rock by a member of a gang who mistook her for a rival gang member. Many violent criminals do not care much about their own lives or about the lives of others.

DRUGS AND GUNS

Gunfights and murders in some inner cities are so common that we risk becoming numb to the traumatic impact on the majority of people who live among them, the children and families who are witness to them. Violence thrives where there is a breakdown in the sense of community, of shared values, or of a meaningful stake in society and a chance to hope and dream about opportunities in the future. Drug abuse rises in communities as a reaction to weakened bonds with families and kin, religious and civic associations, schools, and other neighborhood support systems. Even with a decrease in the use of crack, there is an increase in drug-related violence as dealers compete for the smaller market. Bad debts and territorial disputes appear to be driving many of the assaults and homicides, according to Richard Bennet, professor of justice at Washington's American University.[3]

In an effort to better understand the deeply disturbing crisis of violence among our youth, several hearings were held before the House of Representatives Select Committee on Children, Youth and Families in the late 1980s. In the opening statement at one hearing, Representative George Miller, chairman of the committee, noted that the recent surge in youth violence is a tragic culmination of three insidious trends: crack cocaine, an increase in race-related hate crimes among adolescents, and problems associated with poverty.[4] The growing availability of drugs and guns has undoubtedly exacerbated the violence problem. To cite an example of how violence has penetrated American culture, rap music is usually about success derived from violence, power, control, and success.

Both the media and cultural heroes glorify firearms as an easy way to resolve conflicts, with no one appearing to get hurt. One boy, who was shot, expressed surprise about his pain in the emergency room of a hospital. He had not seen the anguish of injury when he watched television.

THE VIOLENCE OF CRACK

In the United States, the number of people using drugs appears to have declined, but drug-related violence still escalates.[5] Some urban neighborhoods have been transformed into war zones for the drug trade. Crack is a drug dealer's dream: it is cheap to make, easily hidden, and provides an intense, short-lived high. The high is followed by a low, or depression, which cocaine users know can be "cured" with another fix. For some people the craving is so severe that they will do anything for more cocaine. One woman sold her child for sex, then went off with her boyfriend to buy cocaine.[6]

Charles V. Wetli, Metropolitan Dade County medical examiner in Miami, describes the violence of cocaine on users in a different way. Although deaths from allergic reactions to cocaine are relatively infrequent, Dr. Wetli believes that cocaine fatalities will continue to develop until there is widespread realization that cocaine is not a harmless drug—it kills.[7]

In addition to random killings in cocaine wars, murder for profit to buy cocaine, and allergic reactions, cocaine also kills in another, albeit indirect, way: through domestic violence. Many concerned people ask if six-year-old Lisa Steinberg might still be alive if her adoptive parents had not been freebasing cocaine the

61

night she was fatally battered. Although each of these situations is the result of complex factors, drugs played a part in the violence. They are examples of the some of the worst scenarios, but crack violence permeates many communities where drug bazaars openly invite buyers. If the drug bazaars are closed down by police, dealers just move to another place.

Not everyone who tries cocaine becomes addicted to it, but crack is known to be one of the most addicting and dangerous of all illegal drugs. The mere sight of a crack pipe or a drug dealer can trigger an uncontrollable urge to smoke the drug. Users lie, steal, cheat, deal in drugs, and commit other criminal acts to obtain more crack. The depression that is part of the cycle can be so profound that some users have been known to commit suicide.

GANGS AND CRACK

Selling crack is a billion-dollar business. New reports that estimate as many as 5 million current users make it clear that the market is large.[8] Even if the crack epidemic is showing signs of decreasing, drugs and violence remain. As babies grow into children on these mean streets, they are drawn into the drug scene by dealers who have no qualms about creating new addicts. They see the drug trade as so lucrative that it is worth killing for, and many users appear indifferent to the use of deadly force. Victims can be gunned down at close range in public because witnesses are afraid to testify. Rival gangs kill easily for their share in the drug market. At one time there was a code of honor among thieves, but these controls have all but disappeared. Today whatever you can get is the rule of the street.

Much of the trade is controlled by gangs whose members range in age from seven- and eight-year-olds to "old gangsters" in their twenties. Many gangs are loosely organized, while others are highly structured. Gang members identify their allegiance by hand signals, the colors and kind of clothing they wear, and the side of the body on which they wear their insignia. Caps with gang insignia have been sold in legal markets.

Some gang leaders have made large sums of money, which they use to buy flashy cars, expensive clothing, heavy gold jewelry, and gold caps for their teeth. Along with displaying their wealth, they display their violent minds through their actions. For example, one group of youths in Washington, D.C., robbed, gang-raped, and murdered a 99-pound (44.5-kg) middle-aged mother while laughing and joking. In another case, a seventeen-year-old shot an unsuspecting cab driver in the head because "he wanted to try out a gun."

Numerous gang members have been in and out of prison and in and out of hospital emergency rooms with crushed bones and blasted organs. Some of them have died in shootouts before reaching the hospital. Children who start as lookouts for $100 a day often are promoted to the job of runner for three times that salary, and they move on to become wealthy dealers. However, many of them do not live long enough to enjoy their wealth in this world in which there seem to be no rules at all. Many boys in gangs will spend their future as drug addicts and/or some time as prisoners. If runners arrive late, their pay is docked. They may be shot or maimed if they are suspected of cheating. One who gets caught stealing a little crack for himself or herself may be shot in the kneecaps. The crack business has been compared to a modern brutalized version of the nineteenth-century sweatshops.[9]

Young people are lured into the drug business as lookers and runners. Consider the case of Juan Jason Vega, a thirteen-year-old who was found dead on a couch in the front room of an apartment that was used for drug dealing. A few envelopes filled with cocaine and some plastic bags and tinfoil, often used to package cocaine for street sales, were nearby. A 9-mm machine pistol was found near his body. Jason (the name he used) was described by neighbors as a "good person" who did not like school but who stayed away from "bad kids." Many believed he had been sucked into the drug trade despite efforts of relatives to steer him away. Neighbors were upset that drug dealers could kill a "little kid," even though they had long since accepted the violence brought by drug trading as a part of life.[10]

For some boys and girls, becoming a gang member begins as a way of survival and then becomes a way of life. The following is taken from Ismael Huerta's oral and prepared statements before the House Select Committee on Children, Youth and Families, March 9, 1988:

I got involved in gangs for the reason that all my friends were doing it. It was the thing and I regret it now because I can't go nowhere without being followed by rival gang members.

I've been shot at many times. I've never been hit. The reason I came here was to tell you guys what it's really like out on the streets.

Where I come from, most of the gang members sell drugs to get weapons. The weapons we use are automatic rifles, machine guns, Uzis. A couple of my friends have grenades.

I started getting involved in gangs when I was 15. . . . We hang out on street corners drinking beer. Some of my friends send me drugs to get loaded on.

I don't go to school. I dropped out for the reason that I was involved in a gang and I was getting harassed by other gang members in that school. . . . One of my friends got stabbed and shot while I was there. So they kicked us out of school and sent us to a continuation school, which is worse because that is where they send all the gang members, and you get put in with rival gang members. So I dropped out because I was tired of getting messed with, and the school said they were tired of messing with us.

If I was to start all over, I would never have gotten in this. The reason I don't want to be in a gang any more is because I can't go out to other places unless it's my neighborhood. I would get messed with if I went by myself, so when I go away from Lennox [the name of his gang], there's always ten of us, and one of us always has a gun or we aren't going anywhere.

Another reason is the way it affected my younger brother. He decided to do the same thing I did. He was 14, and he started getting messed with because he was my brother. . . .

Another reason I can't get ahead in this world is because of my appearance. They think that just because I am a gang member, I'll probably rob them. If I do get a job, I'll get messed with by another gang if they find I work there.

That happened with my last job. Three rival gang members found out where I worked and chased me around the building. One of the guys had a knife. I was working at a lawyer's office, filing and running copies. If I do have a job, it's got to be in my neighborhood.

That's why most of my friends sell drugs. We'd get money to buy guns to protect ourselves from other people. I don't sell drugs anymore. Now I help out my friends and cousins, painting. When I do get money, I give it to my mother. I live with my mother and my father, three brothers and one sister. My dad works, and my dad believes I should be a responsible adult. But when I do get money, they ask if it's from drugs. If it is, they say they don't want dirty money. That's why I have to do it right.[11]

Ismael was being helped by Youth Gang Services, which includes former gang members who have lived with the violence and survived. They try to get people like him involved in sports and other activities, but budget cuts make their jobs especially difficult. Social workers and police are competing with the pull of a drug trade that provides easy money for clothes, cars, jewelry, guns, and power. Many young people are willing to take the risks that are involved. They see dealing as the only way out of their poverty.

Dealers defend their turf with a wide variety of guns. Black-market Uzi submachine guns and Russian-made AK-47 assault rifles are part of their arsenals, along with rifles, handguns, shotguns, and knives. Ironically, many of them have arsenals larger than the police forces that try to protect the communities from gang violence.

SCHOOLS: THE NEXT BATTLEGROUND

In a period of fifteen days in the summer of 1990, six children were hit by stray bullets in New York City, some in their own homes. That very summer, there were thirteen shooting deaths and seventy-five incidents of violence in a single weekend in Chicago as the result of drugs, gangs, arguments, and drive-by shootings.[12]

Some of the students who attend public high schools in New York City routinely carry weapons along with their books because they fear for their safety as they travel to and from school. Transit Authority police began escorting high school students on designated subway cars in Brooklyn, New York, early in May 1990. Even in schools that are considered safe, there have been incidents of violence.[13]

In many areas, robberies and assault inside the schools seem to have declined in the past five years; however, an increase of violence against elementary school teachers was reported recently in New York City.[14] The introduction of hand-held metal detectors for use by security guards, who randomly check students as they enter some schools in New York, is credited with a decrease in violence in public high schools.

Although conditions have improved, there are now schools that resemble armed camps, with police guards posted outside and armed guards inside. Many parents dread phone calls from the principal because they fear hearing that their children have been injured rather than hearing that they have failed academically. Teachers in some schools are suspicious of students who wear bulky coats because they might be hiding guns, either for self-defense or for use in a drug war. Carrying a gun is somewhat similar to smoking at a gas station. The chances are low that an explosion will happen, but all of the ingredients for tragedy are there.

Even young children who are not involved in the drug scene are affected by the atmosphere of violence. In the Bronx, in New York City, a kindergarten student had a gun in the lunchroom. The teacher thought it was a toy pistol, and since toys were not permitted in the lunchroom, the teacher took it away—only to find that it was a loaded gun. In certain schools in Omaha, Nebraska, employees learn code words and hand signals that allow them to tell one another unobtrusively to call the police.

In Orange County, California, large plastic passes are issued to school visitors so that they will be distinguishable from strangers who might be carrying drugs or guns. In Houston, Texas, and Little Rock, Arkansas, mobile units can go quickly to any school in the district in an emergency. The Los Angeles School District has its own police force, from which one or two officers are posted at nearly every secondary school, and about thirty officers are on rotation among elementary schools.

Despite these precautions, fear of violence prevails in many schools. For example, tens of thousands of students stayed away from New York City high schools on Halloween after there were sprees of terror and violence at the end of the previous school day.[15] Halloween pranks have included setting hundreds of fires in abandoned buildings, breaking windows, and trashing property in supermarkets, restaurants, department stores, and other shops. Gangs of boys and girls have mugged people on the street, sending some to hospital emergency rooms.[16] Certainly, many students live in fear of violence every day of the year.

GUNS ON THESE MEAN STREETS

The drug wars have shattered thousands of decent black families and destroyed the peace of mind of millions of people in cities and countryside. Imagine growing up in an area where drug use, illegitimacy, divorce, and abandonment are commonplace and the fear of street violence rules life. Gunfire is so common that you duck into a building or hit the ground when you hear it. People are afraid to trust their neighbors, and they retreat behind bolted doors. The fistfights of ten years ago are gunfights today, and these gunfights may begin with something as simple as losing a place in line at a grocery store or a movie.

The noise of semiautomatic weapons and ambulances are familiar sounds on street corners in many cities throughout the United States. In areas known as "crack heaven," the dead are carried out in body bags. Where crack houses have spread to the suburbs, drug-related violence has followed.

Fear of violence infects whole communities to the degree that people suffer from something similar to battle fatigue as a result of constant stress. In a typical week, a drug dealer drives slowly down the street and fires shots at people on the sidewalk. A woman is killed while talking on a pay telephone. A boy is killed while going to the store for a loaf of bread. Even those who stay indoors are not entirely safe from the urban wars fought over drug turf.

Some adults complain that they worry about being shot even when they are putting out the garbage. They have learned telltale signs that a shooting is about to start. If a car is moving beyond a normal speed, or is moving very slowly, they get out of the way. Most people look both ways before they cross a street. In drug war zones, people look both ways before they *get* to the street.

Although there have always been drugs in their neighborhood, the crack epidemic has changed the frequency and amount of the violence, so even children who are not involved with drugs are influenced by the underground drug economy.

Researchers who study the effect of crack on young people in a community believe that children and teens feel that they have to be tough so as not to be picked on. They say that crack has created a new model of behavior in which youths have enormous power, even over the older generation. Some teens sell crack to adults, including to their parents, thus rupturing the normal line of parental authority. However, gang leaders as well as gang members can come from fairly stable families.

THE CHANGING SCENE

In 1990, several politicians in Detroit, Michigan, believed that the city no longer faced a serious gang problem. But new research published in *Dangerous Places,* a book by criminologist Carl Taylor, shows that the gangs have grown into sophisticated, secret business operations. These dealers do not display their wealth by wearing gold chains and driving expensive cars. They prefer to be less visible in their casual street clothes. Like the old gangs, they draw recruits from the impoverished, but the new covert enterprises are luring members of middle-class families with the promise of quick financial rewards. Even groups of women work with these operations, and they too are willing to kill to further their careers. Carl Taylor urges an all-out war on poverty, unemployment, and the inferior education that make the urban underclass a seedbed for violence and crime.[17]

The drug scene has had an impact on the criminal justice system. Although they have long been overloaded, today's courts are swamped with drug cases. Prisons are so overcrowded that large numbers of felons get off with no jail time at all because there is no space for them. In Georgia, for example, four of every five crimes are drug-related, and even hardened criminals must be released after short sentences due to overcrowded prisons. In New York City, about 2 million warrants are out for defendants and others who were supposed to appear before the overcrowded, understaffed criminal justice system.[18]

Even if drug dealing were to disappear, violence would continue in these mean streets. Many of the fights are between two individuals who know each other and who have been drinking. The problem may start with something as simple as whose turn it is to clean the cat's litter pan. Violence begins when angry storekeepers shoot at burglars, when lovers quarrel, and in countless other ways. But the majority of homicides occur between two young men of the same race who know each other, who have been drinking, who get into an argument (often over a relatively minor issue), and one of whom is carrying a weapon. The violent action is spontaneous, making it unlikely that the consequences of criminal justice are taken into consideration before the violent behavior leads to injury or death. Even if there were space to confine all of the drug users and dealers, some violence would continue. Many thoughtful citizens, as well as drug prevention experts, are rethinking new strategies in combatting the violence on these mean streets.

VIOLENCE AND POVERTY

It is increasingly clear that poverty puts people at greater risk for violence. Black homicide rates are six to twelve times higher than white rates. According to Howard Spivak, deputy commissioner of the Massachusetts Department of Public Health, the overrepresentation of blacks in the violence and homicide statistics reflects their overrepresentation in poverty. Studies that have corrected homicide rates for socioeconomic status have found that racial differences in these rates disappear when poverty is taken into account.[19]

Much of America cannot relate to the lives of families who live among this violence. For example, sickness is a big problem. Although many poor people continue to struggle to stay healthy, they lack money for transportation and access to medical care even in the most overcrowded, understaffed medical centers. In Mississippi, for example, more than half of the doctors practice in just eight counties.[20] In some rural areas of the United States, open sewers flood homes, rats and roaches are commonplace, and there are no inside toilet facilities. Rats and roaches also add to the problems of poorly educated, job-seeking city dwellers who live on the mean streets ruled by the violence of live-fast, die-fast drug dealers and their customers.

The violence on the streets is destroying families and ravaging the health of children and adults alike, but many of the poor do manage to rise above the conditions they grew up in.

Although an increasing number of the young are refusing to try crack, violence persists. There are no easy answers to violence prevention, but the situation is so serious that responses to the challenge of creating a less violent world come from many fronts.

MURDER: THE ULTIMATE VIOLENCE

Murder has always held a morbid fascination for people, and murder mysteries have always been a popular form of entertainment. During the Elizabethan era, in sixteenth-century England, people flocked to see performances of gory plays that were dramatized versions of real crimes. The plays were known as domestic tragedies, and they reflected the kinds of murders committed at that time, usually motivated by money or passion.[1] Eager audiences of today relish the sensational details of the latest murder with as much enthusiasm as those of earlier times. One of the reasons for this appetite for gruesome events is that reading about murder or watching a horror film is a safe way of experiencing thrills and fright vicariously.

THEORIES ABOUT WHY PEOPLE KILL

There are many theories about why and when people began killing each other, but no one really knows. According to archaeologist Raymond Dart, more than 2 million years ago, one of our humanoid ancestors, called *Australopithecus*, became very adept at smashing the skulls of other animals such as baboons, as well as those of fellow humanoids. As meat eaters, they crushed the skulls in order to extract the brains for food. Dart's evidence was based on fossils found in Africa, Asia, and the South Seas.[2] Peking man, who lived about half a million years ago, also practiced cannibalism. In addition, archeologists have discovered ancient skeletons (more males than females), that show clear evidence of injury by stabbing, usually on the left side, indicating that the attacker was right-handed. Some remains even contain fragments of the weapon.[3]

In the book *A Criminal History of Man,* writer Colin Wilson comments that the development of xenophobia (literally, fear of strangers) among primitive people may have marked the beginning of criminality and killing. When humans began thinking in terms of "us" and "them" and depersonalizing outsiders, it became easier to kill them. The same holds true today.[4]

Human beings have been killing each other for a long time, and the earliest written records contain descriptions of wars. But despite the warfare, some ancient civilizations were quite humane and moral. The earliest recorded murder trial, found in Sumerian writings, took place nearly 4,000 years ago.[5]

KINDS OF MURDER

As civilizations have changed, patterns of homicide and attitudes about criminality have changed as well. In seventh century England, murder was dealt with by the payment of monetary compensation to the victim's kin, and revenge killing was acceptable under some circumstances.[6] Many cultures, both past and present, consider the killing of an adulterer by a husband as justifiable homicide, and therefore not a criminal act. Even in the United States and other countries where this kind of killing is a crime, prosecutors and juries tend to be sympathetic and more lenient toward men who kill under these circumstances.[7]

The reasons for homicide are complex, and each case is different. To understand this kind of violence more fully, researchers in the twentieth century have drawn from the fields of psychiatry, psychology, sociology, anthropology, law, and philosophy.

73

The motivation for some killings is obvious; money, passion, and politics are common reasons. As noted in previous chapters, most homicides are spontaneous, triggered by the passion of the moment, a lovers' quarrel, or an argument between friends. Some killing is precipitated by alcohol or other drugs, such as PCP. Other murders are coldly premeditated.

Terrorists kill primarily for religious or political causes, but they sometimes kill for money as well. The state itself may be an instrument of murder, as in the case of Nazi Germany, where millions of Jews, Gypsies, and other so-called undesirables were eliminated for political reasons.

Ordinary people can kill under extraordinary circumstances. In his book *Violent Men,* Hans Toch comments that "the carnage of war—terrifyingly standardized and dehumanized and organized—has become an almost non-controversial feature of the human landscape."[8] Under these circumstances, soldiers kill because they are trained to follow orders and are required to destroy the enemy. They are indoctrinated to regard their opponents as objects to be eliminated, and they gain no satisfaction from this kind of violence. The exceptions are some violence-prone individuals who seek out military service to fulfill their own needs in a way that is socially acceptable in time of war. These people often encounter serious problems in adjusting to civilian life.[9]

Sometimes a seriously disturbed person kills another while in a psychotic state. Bill was a young man who had been diagnosed as mentally ill several years earlier because his thinking was confused and he sometimes heard voices. One day, while he was walking through the park, he heard a voice telling him to kill a young woman who was sitting on a bench eating her lunch. The voice told him that the woman was evil, and it was so commanding and insistent that he felt compelled to obey. He struck her head against a wall and killed her. Bill was found not guilty by reason of insanity, and he was committed to the state mental hospital, where he received treatment and supervision for his mental illness. Unfortunately, this kind of crime is widely publicized and sensationalized in the media, with the result that most people are led to believe that all mentally ill individuals are dangerous and violent. On the contrary, numerous studies have concluded that mentally ill people are no more likely to commit violent acts than anyone else.[10]

In addition, many people think that the insanity defense is used too often and frequently is a successful maneuver that allows wrongdoers to avoid prison. This perception is false. Data gathered in Maryland showed that only 1.2 percent of 11,497 defendants in Baltimore superior court during 1984–1985 used this defense. It was successful in only fourteen of the cases, and the prosecution and defense agreed on most of those. Only two defendants actually had full trials.[11] Unusual and shocking cases that are overplayed and exploited by the media, like that of John Hinckley's attempt to assassinate President Reagan, leave the impression that killers can literally get away with murder.

Most killers are not insane. Insanity is not a term used by psychiatrists; it is a legal term. One would be considered insane under the law if judged to lack substantial capacity to appreciate the criminality of one's conduct or to conform that conduct to the requirements of the law. In Bill's case, he did not understand that he was doing something wrong when he hit the young woman, and he was unable to resist the power of the commanding voice.

CLASSIFICATIONS OF MURDER

Various researchers have proposed a number of classifications for murder.[12] Emmanuel Tanay divided murderers into three categories, which he termed psychotic, dissociative, and ego-syntonic. The psychotic type is driven by delusional thinking that may overcome normal cultural controls. The dissociative murderer kills in a state of altered consciousness, different from his or her normal personality; this kind of murder may be precipitated by a very stressful event, or by one of the mind-altering drugs, such as PCP. On the other hand the ego-syntonic type of murder is a purposeful act, consciously acceptable and rational to the perpetrator.

Many violent individuals perceive the world as threatening, and they respond to certain situations with violence as a matter of course.

However, many murders are committed by people who were described by friends and family as quiet, studious, mild-mannered, and gentle—with no previous propensity for violence. Psychologist Edwin Megargee divided violence-prone individuals into two general categories: the undercontrolled assaultive type and the overcontrolled assaultive type.[13] James Huberty appeared to have gone berserk with little or no warning. He became despondent and angry over the loss of his job and his failure to find other work. One day, armed with guns and ammunition, he walked to the local McDonald's restaurant and gunned down everyone in sight, killing a total of twenty-one people.[14]

Another example is Harry. Harry was a disappointment to his father, because he was not a very good student and was rejected by West Point and Annapolis. He was admitted to a private military academy, and he went reluctantly, under pressure from his father. He did not do well at college and was not popular with his fellow students. Feeling like a total failure and brooding about his father's constant pushing, he left school to go home for Thanksgiving. Harry could not bring himself to discuss his feelings with his father. Instead, he took a pistol, went to the bedroom where his parents were sleeping, and shot his father and then his mother. Next he shot both of his brothers.

Harry and the man who gunned down the people at McDonald's clearly had some psychological problems, but neither had shown any propensity for violence in the past. They both fit the category of the overcontrolled type of individual; they kept their emotions bottled up, so the pressure built to unbearable limits. The stressful situations in their lives triggered their violent explosions.

Rick was the oldest of ten children whose father was an alcoholic. He was neglected and often physically abused by both parents. He began stealing at an early age, was sent to prison for armed robbery at seventeen, and continued his criminal activities after his release. When he was twenty-one years old, during an attempt to rob a liquor store, he shot and killed the owner in order to prevent him from reaching for the telephone. Rick is an example of the under-controlled assaultive type of murderer. These individuals are lacking in self-restraint and generally have a history of aggressive and antisocial behavior.

SERIAL MURDER

The most bizarre and frightening killer of all is the kind of mass murderer typified by Edward Gein. He was a quiet, middle-aged loner who lived in rural Wisconsin. At the start of deer season in 1957, the owner of the local hardware store returned from hunting and discovered that his mother was missing. A subsequent investigation led the police to Gein's farm, where they came upon a grisly sight. Hanging in the barn, trussed up like a deer, with a rod inserted through her ankles, was the headless body of the missing woman. The body had been slit open and all of the internal organs had been removed.

Further investigation revealed that Gein had butchered and dismembered other victims in the past and also had stolen bodies from graves. In his home was a gruesome collection of body parts, some of which he had made into decorations and pieces of clothing. None of his neighbors could believe that this quiet man was capable of committing such dreadful acts, nor could they understand why. The sickening story of Edward Gein's bizarre killings is said to have been the inspiration for several horror films, including Alfred Hitchcock's *Psycho*.[15]

In 1977, the people of Los Angeles were terrorized by a series of brutal murders. Within a five-month period, the nude bodies of ten young women were found on hillsides and along roads. All had been tortured, raped, and strangled. The so-called Hillside Strangler turned out to be two cousins, Kenneth Bianchi and Angelo Buono, who carefully and cold-bloodedly planned their acts of murder.[16]

The first few victims were prostitutes; then the cousins went on to kill young students, torturing them in an increas-

77

ingly brutal manner. It was later discovered that they posed as police officers, making it easier to lure their prey.

Although the police pursued thousands of leads, the crimes remained unsolved until a year later, when Kenneth Bianchi was arrested in Bellingham, Washington, for the rape and murder of two college students. His friends could not believe that he was capable of killing anyone; they described him as a nice guy. His boss considered him a reliable worker. His girl friend, who was also the mother of his baby, said that he was gentle and kind.

Angelo Buono owned an auto upholstery shop. He had been married three times and had several children. Although he had a record of petty crimes and was known as a pimp and an abuser of the prostitutes who worked for him, he, like Kenneth Bianchi, appeared rather ordinary on the surface.

What triggered their killing spree? One weak explanation is that Ken and Angelo had a discussion about how it would feel to kill someone; then they decided to see for themselves.

The Germans have a term for this kind of murder: joy-murder, or murder for pleasure, in contrast to the kind of crime that author Colin Wilson calls business-murder, or killing with a motive.[17] The killers described above are the joy-murderers, the serial killers, who have no obvious motives and whose activities are almost impossible to detect.

Serial murder is not really a new phenomenon. Nearly 2,000 years ago, the Roman emperor Caligula killed for pleasure. In the fifteenth century, the French nobleman Gilles de Rais sexually abused and murdered 140 children. And almost everyone has heard of the famous English murderer Jack the Ripper, who lived in the late nineteenth century.[18]

More recently, however, concern about the menace of serial murder has grown, because these killings have been increasing at an alarming rate since 1960, according to the FBI.[19] It is estimated that there were at least 500 serial killers at large in the United States in the late 1980s. These murderers are the most sinister of all of the violent criminals because they usually appear ordinary and their behavior is socially acceptable. In contrast to other mass murderers, they kill their victims one by one. John Gacy was a respected member of the community and a successful businessman who had been nominated for the Man of the Year award by the local chapter of the Jaycees. He even had his picture taken with First Lady Rosalynn Carter at a Democratic party meeting. Gacy was later discovered to have killed thirty-three boys.[20]

There are countless unsolved homicides and cases of missing people throughout the country, and many of them are eventually found to be victims of serial killers. The 260 serial killers studied by one researcher had killed a total of more than 10,000 people.[21] It is extremely difficult for the authorities to connect the victims with an unknown killer who leaves no clues to his identity. A pattern linking the murders to one killer may not become obvious for months or years. In addition, the murderer often moves to another part of the country to continue his killings, making discovery even more difficult. A national network, organized in the 1980s, is now coordinating the efforts of local authorities and the FBI to track these crimes more efficiently.

Serial killers are different from other murderers; they are literally addicted to killing. Some feel guilty immediately after killing their victims, and they desperately wish to be stopped. One murderer left a message scrawled on a mirror with lipstick; it said, "Stop me before I do it again." Others leave clues to help the police find them.

Serial murderers are obsessed with their secret fantasies, carefully planning and acting out the crime in their minds, even though at the same time they may be living ordinary lives and behaving normally. Under the compulsion to act on their fantasy, they begin to go "trolling" for their next victim. Some killers choose prostitutes; others look for young boys; each usually has a special preference. The killer may identify a particular person and stalk that person like prey for some time before actually striking. Some pick up unsuspecting hitchhikers. Ted Bundy was a good-looking, charming part-time law student who sometimes pretended he had a broken arm so that his female victims had no qualms about helping him.[22]

When the killer has finally trapped a victim, he performs the murder in a ritual of violence that often includes torture, mutilation, and sexual abuse. Many experience a "high" or a sexual release at the moment of killing their victims.

It is very difficult to comprehend how human beings can carry out such horrendous acts of violence. According to Drs. Eugene Revitch and Louis B. Schlesinger, most compulsive murderers are driven by sexual conflicts.[23]

Most serial murderers are men. Although women have committed brutal and sadistic murders, they very seldom commit this kind of crime.[24] Many serial killers were severely abused or deprived in childhood and have grown up with a deep sense of inadequacy and powerlessness. Killing may be one way to acquire power. When the police search for a serial killer, they look for men who hate their mothers or sisters or who feel wronged by their wives or girl friends. They may feel guilty about sex, and they may be preoccupied with incestuous thoughts. These are men who want to control and hurt women.

Most are not legally insane. They are antisocial individuals who wear the mask of sanity. They have no regard for their victims and have dehumanized them. Henry Lee Lucas, who murdered countless people, is said to have described the murders the way most people describe the weather.

IDENTIFYING FUTURE KILLERS

Experts have tried to find a basis for predicting future criminal behavior by assembling a typical profile. They examine the past histories and the physical and psychological makeup of murderers, even including physical characteristics such as malformed ears and bulbous fingertips, which might signal genetic defects. Many killers have a history of assault, deviant sexual behavior, and other behavior such as bed-wetting, fire setting, and cruelty to animals. Some show evidence of brain injury or other neurological problems. But this approach may not be much more helpful than that of Lombroso, who claimed the ability to identify criminal types by the configuration of their heads.

Generally, studying a small group of violent offenders is not very useful as a predictor of violence in people. It is not surprising to find that the most violent offenders were abused in childhood or have shown deviant behavior in the past, such as cruelty to animals. But these studies say nothing about the prevalence of such behavior or characteristics in the general population. Although there are millions of abused children, relatively few grow up to be violent adults.

Experts agree that further research is needed to identify more accurately those individuals who are prone to violence. A myriad of factors in the environment and in the makeup of the individual play a role in triggering violent behavior, so it may never be possible to target every potential killer. Researchers hope that with early detection of those most at risk, intervention can take place at a younger age and perhaps decrease the chances that the children identified will grow up to become violent.

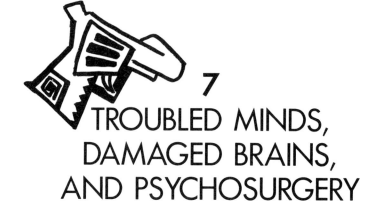

7
TROUBLED MINDS, DAMAGED BRAINS, AND PSYCHOSURGERY

In their search for causes of violence, psychiatrists, psychologists, sociologists, and others have looked carefully at troubled minds and damaged brains.

For a number of years, many surgeons thought they had found an excellent answer to the cause of violence and the control of violent minds, as well as many other varieties of mental illness. This answer was psychosurgery, an operation in which healthy brain tissue was destroyed to control the emotions or behavior of difficult patients, even though there was no apparent brain disease. Although the operations usually resulted in taming the violent patient, there were other results, too.

EARLY EXPERIMENTS

Consider the case of Oretha, a large woman who was so strong that it took five attendants to drag her from the "strong room" in the mental hospital, where she had been confined for years, in preparation for her operation. Oretha weighed 300 pounds (135 kg) and was a violent person whose actions understandably had frightened the staff. After Dr. Walter Freeman, an early advocate of psychosurgery, destroyed a section of her brain, Oretha became quite docile. Dr. Freeman illustrated this to the timorous ward personnel on a number of occasions by grabbing Oretha by the throat and tickling her in the ribs. Before the operation, Oretha would have lashed out in fury, but now she reacted only with a wide grin or a hoarse chuckle.[1]

One of Dr. Freeman's patients was a very troublesome six-year-old child. The child's parents complained about her destructive behavior, which included smashing her toys. The girl was subjected to various treatments, including two operations in which some brain tissue was destroyed. After the operations, she was withdrawn but less troublesome. In a follow-up several years after the operation, Dr. Freeman reported that the girl was easily managed at home in spite of her increased speed and strength. Her impulsive, destructive behavior was subsiding, and she was beginning to put sentences together.

These cases of psychosurgery and many that followed were based on the experiments of a famous and well-respected neurosurgeon, Dr. Egas Moniz of Lisbon, Portugal. The frontal lobes of the brain are involved in the process of thinking and planning, as well as other functions. Dr. Moniz believed that serious mental diseases were the result of "fixed" thoughts that interfered with normal mental life. By destroying these abnormally "stabilized" pathways in the frontal lobes of the brain, Moniz believed that he could relieve the patient's mental disturbance.[2]

The first record of such an operation was in the 1890s, when a Swiss doctor, Gottlieb Burckhard, boldly removed parts of the brains of six patients, one of whom died. Several of the patients became easier to manage on the wards, but his experiments were severely criticized by his fellow physicians. There was a great outcry against the destruction of healthy brain tissue, and few operations of this kind were performed until the mid-1930s.[3]

In 1935, when Moniz pioneered leucotomy, or lobotomy as it came to be known in the United States, doctors around the world were searching for ways to treat, or even to handle, patients with serious mental illness. Institutions that held the incurably insane were known as "snake pits" because of the inhumane treatment of the patients. In spite of efforts to improve the terrible conditions, there was a lack of knowledge about how to provide effective treatment, and improvements languished. Many thousands of mentally ill people lived in wretched conditions for years in crowded buildings, naked and living in their own filth. Caretakers explained that patients tore the clothing from their bodies and refused to follow rules that would permit any semblance of sanitation.

During the years before the introduction of tranquilizers, many desperate and bizarre remedies were employed to treat a wide variety of mental problems. Knowledge about the functioning of the brain and the causes of mental disease was extremely limited, and confinement in strong rooms seemed the best solution for people with violent minds.

WIDESPREAD USE
OF LOBOTOMIES

The introduction of lobotomies produced docile patients. Patients became subdued and easier to manage. Some were able to go home to live with their families, and there were reports that some could work at menial jobs. But there were many negative reports, too. Lobotomy impairs the highest human centers for empathy, understanding, abstract reasoning, and future planning. Although the violence and other unpleasant characteristics were removed, these first lobotomies left patients in a state of apathy.[4]

Although some patients seemed to improve, many deteriorated over the long term. Advocates pointed out that lobotomies performed on hopeless patients provided a tremendous financial advantage to taxpayers. Fewer patients had to live at the state hospitals, and those who did were easier to manage. This encouraged many individuals to overlook the fact that these patients were being robbed of their creativity and sense of self. In their efforts to control the violence in custodial institutions, many doctors were willing to fool themselves into believing that their patients were being helped by the lobotomies.

In its early form, a lobotomy involved the destruction of a portion of the frontal lobe of the brain. It was thus known as a prefrontal lobotomy.[5] In the first type of operation devised by Dr. Moniz, a neurosurgeon drilled two holes in the skull of a mental patient, and absolute alcohol was injected into the frontal lobes of the brain. The alcohol destroyed some of the brain tissue, permanently altering the personality of the patient. After five more similar procedures, this operation was modified so that the surgeon used an ice pick type of instrument, instead of alcohol, to destroy nerve cells.[6]

Prefrontal lobotomies became a popular form of treatment from the mid-1930s through the mid-1950s. Despite the objections of many doctors in the field, prefrontal lobotomies were performed in a number of different countries. Dr. Freeman himself is reported to have performed about 3,500 such operations.[7] The technique was used to treat a wide variety of symptoms, ranging from long-term psychosis (a condition in which patients are out of touch with reality) to drug addiction and uncontrollable behavior in children. After the operations, most patients lived an emotionally flat, subdued existence. Dr. Freeman noted that it was the ideal operation for use in crowded state mental hospitals with a shortage of everything except patients.[8]

After World War II, the practice of psychosurgery increased in many countries around the world. The media proclaimed its wonders. One headline, which appeared in *Life* magazine in 1947, read: "Psychosurgery: Operation to Cure Sick Minds Turns Surgeon's Blade into an Instrument of Mental Therapy." The technique was viewed as anything from a cure for violence to "murder of the mind."[9] Although doctors disagreed among themselves about the use of psychosurgery, many of their criticisms did not reach the public.

Doctors noted that the results of prefrontal lobotomies varied greatly with different individuals, depending somewhat on the patient's problems, the quality of the operation itself, as well as the aftercare each patient received, and the reactions of those who evaluated them. Many violent and anxious patients did experience relief from their symptoms. In the worst cases, patients deteriorated into a completely demented state.[10]

IMPROVING TECHNIQUES IN PSYCHOSURGERY

In efforts to improve results, surgeons shifted from the technique in which they cut nerve fibers in the prefrontal lobes of the brain to another area, the limbic system, which is seated much deeper inside the brain. Experiments had shown that the destruction of any part of the limbic system readily alters the behavior of animals. The area on which most attention was centered was the portion known as the amygdala (see diagram, The Human Brain, on page 26). This is the part that is most strongly identified with rage, violence, and aggression.

New techniques enabled surgeons to reach the limbic system and to destroy less tissue. Drs. Vernon H. Mark and Frank R. Ervin became famous for their operations on the amygdala. They used stereotactic surgery, a technique in which tiny electrodes are implanted in the brain and activated to destroy a very small number of cells in an area that could be more precisely determined than was possible in previous methods.[11]

Although prefrontal lobotomies were performed on members of affluent families as well as in state institutions, both the serious adverse effects of surgery and the advent of tranquilizers played a part in greatly reducing the number of lobotomies performed. Today new techniques and careful screening of candidates precede any tissue destruction, but there are cases in which psychosurgery is still recommended.

For example, one of the most tragic conditions related to violent behavior is Lesch-Nyhan syndrome. Those who suffer from it are usually normal, or nearly normal, in intelligence, but they suffer episodes of self-destruction. If not restrained, they may bite off their lips, tongues, fingers, and chunks of flesh. In such cases, doctors may recommend stereotactic psychosurgery, although there are relatively few conditions in which doctors try to excise violence with the knife today.

VIOLENCE AND BRAIN ABNORMALITIES

While admitting that social forces can play a part in generating violent behavior, many neurosurgeons, such as Drs. Mark and Ervin, were especially concerned about violent individuals who suffered from abnormal brain function. Although Drs. Mark and Ervin acknowledged that only a small percentage of patients with brain disease and associated violent behavior required surgery, their proposal to screen individuals with poor control of impulsive behavior came under considerable criticism.

In their claims about the prevalence of brain disease in violent individuals, Mark and Ervin cite the case of Charles Whitman who shot forty-one people, most of them from his perch on the University of Texas tower in Austin, Texas, on August 1, 1966.[12] Whitman was an honor student who had told a psychiatrist that he had "forced thoughts" about climbing the tower and killing many students with a rifle. Whitman suffered from a highly malignant brain tumor that could have been detected by a routine brain examination, but this was not discovered until after he was killed by policemen's bullets that stopped his eighty-minute rampage. Richard Speck, the man who murdered eight nurses in Chicago, Lee Harvey Oswald, who assassinated President Kennedy, and many other destructive, violent people have been identified as having had brain abnormalities.

Drs. Mark and Ervin claimed that the number of potentially violence-prone individuals in the United States might run into millions.[13] Their estimate that 5 to 10 percent of the population have brains that do not function normally and their theory about the relationship of organic brain disease to violence have been called unsubstantiated and controversial. Dr. Elliot S. Valenstein states that "there is no convincing evidence that . . . episodically occurring violence caused by brain pathology represents anything more than a very insignificant percentage of the violence in our society."[14]

The great majority of people who have brain damage and who suffer from mental illness are not violent. When a mentally ill person does commit a violent crime, sensational media coverage leads many readers to overestimate the connection between mental illness and violence.

Some severe mental disorders are linked to abnormalities in the brain, yet all mentally ill people continue to be stigmatized. Only 10 percent of the people polled in a recent survey thought that severe mental illness had a biological basis and involved the brain. With new scientific technology, doctors can see structure and activity in living human brains, and this has provided graphic evidence that some conditions are associated with brain dysfunction. For example, exquisitely detailed pictures of the brain made by using a technique called magnetic resonance have shown brain abnormalities in autistic children and in schizophrenic patients. Such disorders were once attributed to poor parenting.[15]

Most scientists now believe that schizophrenia and other disorders, such as manic-depressive illness, have a biological basis. Many studies have demonstrated that genetics does play a role, and there is strong evidence that alterations of certain biochemical compounds in the body are involved in the development of these illnesses.

SCHIZOPHRENIA AND VIOLENCE

Schizophrenia, the most chronic and disabling of the mental illnesses, afflicts about 1 percent of the adult population, or 1.8 million people within any given six-month period.[16] One form of schizophrenia, paranoid schizophrenia, is most frequently associated with violence. Hearing "voices" that usually consist of derogatory remarks about the patient is characteristic of this form of illness. In rare cases, the voices give "orders" that involve acts of violence. For example, one patient heard voices that ordered him to kill people in order to prevent earthquakes in San Francisco. He was made to believe that committing a murder would protect human beings from earthquakes: "A minor natural disaster avoids a major natural disaster." In less than a year, he created thirteen "minor disasters" by killing thirteen people. Fortunately, the voices of paranoid schizophrenia can be controlled through medication.[17]

THE ANTISOCIAL PERSONALITY

Some violent individuals fit the diagnosis of the antisocial personality, a character disorder characterized by frequent rule violations and aggressive behavior that begins in childhood or early adolescence. These people are also called psychopaths or sociopaths. Although 1 to 3 percent of all adults fit these descriptions, studies show that as many as 80 percent of male felons released from prisons display antisocial personalities.[18]

Robert D. Hare, famous for his work on antisocial personality, hypothesizes that criminal psychopaths may differ from normal people in the way their brain functions are organized.[19] Psychopaths are mentally abnormal in the sense that they have no compassion or true feeling for others. Since they have no conscience, they take what they want without feeling guilt or remorse. Many of them are very clever at manipulating people.

Most children develop a conscience because they wish to attract and preserve love, rather than for fear of punishment. This conscience continues to operate even when there is no fear of immediate punishment, but such is not the case for sociopaths. They never learn to control their impulses, so they seek immediate gratification even though their actions may victimize others.

Although some sociopaths are killers and criminals, only a small percentage are aggressively violent. Many of them can be found in executive boardrooms, in politics, and in any number of respected professions. Sociopaths are charming, clever, irresponsible, immoral, self-assured, and cunning.[20] They seem incapable of loving others and cannot trust anyone but themselves, but they are experts at masking their lack of feelings for others. This makes it so difficult to recognize their lies and manipulations that even psychiatrists can be fooled.

Mental health professionals find it hard to work with patients who have exhibited the characteristics common to antisocial personality disorder. Treatment is difficult because patients cannot form the necessary relationship with therapists, and in some cases, even the experts cannot tell whether or not the patients are telling the truth. Antisocial behavior has been called one of psychiatry's thorniest problems.

Although theories about the causes of psychopathic minds are controversial, many experts believe that lack of love and attachment to a mother during the early years may be one cause. They say that psychopaths cannot love others because they did not learn how to love when they were children. Many psychopaths come from loveless homes, though this is not always the case. The condition has been attributed to genetic, biological, interpersonal, and cultural causes.[21]

Drs. Samuel Yochelson and Stanton Samenow have proposed a widely disputed theory about antisocial personality disorder on the basis of sixteen years of work with criminal patients at St. Elizabeths Hospital in Washington, D.C. They believe that a criminal personality starts early in life as a matter of coping with reality. Criminals make a series of choices by the age of five or six that develop into a life-style in which there is a thinking disorder.

Dr. Samenow believes that the criminal chooses a life of crime, that he rejects society before it rejects him. Dr. Samenow, who continued the studies after the death of Dr. Yochelson, paints a chilling profile in his book *Inside the Criminal Mind.* He points out that the criminals believe that they are entitled to whatever they desire.

Dr. Samenow refutes the widely held beliefs that broken homes, alcoholism or other drug addiction, TV violence, unemployment, or passionate impulses are the causes of crime. He believes that psychopaths are not forced into crime by their peers but choose the companions they like. They are untrustworthy, but they demand that others trust them and they value people to the extent that they can be manipulated. According to these researchers, criminals must be taught new thinking patterns in order to change their way of life. A mind that has no regard for the safety or rights of others cannot be rehabilitated without such a change.[22] While this analysis of the criminal mind has caused considerable dispute, it has drawn attention to the need for more research on the mind of the sociopath.

People with antisocial personalities are known to be sensation seekers. They seek excitement, admiration, and experiences that put them in control in order to escape boredom. One sixteen-year-old sociopath, who fired a shotgun from an apartment window and killed several adults and children on the grounds of an elementary school below, told a newspaper reporter that she did it for the fun of it.[23] Many sociopaths are drug users, perhaps because they seek stimulation to overcome boredom.

There are degrees of psychopathy, and some of them are more amenable to treatment than others. Checklists of characteristics have been developed to help therapists and criminologists determine the severity of psychopathic disturbance. One of the most reliable checklists, developed by Robert Hare, includes the following characteristics: superficial charm, a grandiose sense of self-worth, need for stimulation/proneness to boredom, pathological lying, and lack of remorse.[24]

Who among us will commit violence? There are no easy answers, but certain kinds of damaged brains and troubled minds appear to put people at greater risk. These, in combination with environmental problems, may produce lethal results.

TOWARD A LESS
VIOLENT SOCIETY

"Violence is everywhere, and there is nothing anybody can do about it" is a common statement but not entirely true. In the first place, violence only *seems* to be everywhere. Suppose some creatures from outer space observed Earthlings for a period of time. They might not see a murder, or less violent acts, or any violence at all. If they observed the reasons for violent disputes, many of them would seem trivial, such as violent reactions to jealousy, money matters, or an insult. The whole chain of events leading to a violent outburst may be hidden, but each link makes the person more apt to behave violently. Escalation occurs until there is an explosion.[1] Violence is common, but most human beings have learned to deal with their anger in peaceful ways.

The amount of violence differs greatly from place to place. In areas where crack and other drugs are sold openly, exposure to violence is an everyday affair. In some communities, they refer to dead bodies as "bagged and tagged," and many children are aware that they will not live to middle age. Mr. Peter Martin Commanday, who offers survival courses for teachers in the New York City school system and in other parts of the country, has compiled 400 practical means of survival.[2]

In many parts of the nation, however, teachers are free of any concern about being attacked by students. Even in the worst areas, most teenagers are not crack addicts.[3] Most youths are not violent, and given a choice, they prefer not to be around violence.[4] However, increased awareness of violence throughout the nation than ever before has led to increased efforts to make society less violent.

VIOLENCE: PREVENTION AND CONTROL

Just as there are no easy answers to the causes of violence, preventing violence is a staggering problem, with more questions than there are answers. Violence among men, women, and children is not new. Since the dawn of human history, violence has erupted between individuals, and since that time, there have been efforts to prevent it.

No one knows exactly how and when the first attempts to prevent violence developed, but it is known that they began long ago. One such piece of evidence appears in records that instruct the wrongdoer to offer compensation to the injured party. In the tenth century, one finds compensation for violence in the laws of King Alfred of England, through the payment known as *bot*. "If the big toe be cut off, let ten shillings be paid to him as bot. If it be the second toe, fifteen shillings, if the middlemost toe, nine shillings. If the fourth toe, six shillings. . . ." Some offenses were "botless"; they were punishable by death or mutilation and entailed a forfeiture of the offender's property to the king.[5]

The codes of chivalry in the Middle Ages are believed to have helped bring widespread violence somewhat under control. However, violence remained a popular method of settling disputes in the hundreds of years that followed. Almost every child-rearing tract from antiquity to the eighteenth century recommended the beating of children. Century after century, children, who were physically and emotionally abused, grew up and abused their own children in return.[6] Although child abuse is still common, many parents have learned new ways to discipline

93

their children. Teachers are introducing students to better ways of relating to each other and of controlling anger at home.

One approach to reducing violence is through the use of skill-training curricula tailored to schools. They teach social skills, build self-esteem, and reduce impulsive and aggressive behavior in children. Students learn about anger management by identifying warning signs expressed by body language (body movements) and by practicing ways to calm down when they are angry. They also use role playing to practice dealing with their anger in nonviolent ways.

For example, in a violence prevention program, a student might be asked to pretend that someone pushed him or her in the lunchroom line. Shane takes the part of the person who pushed in the line, and Jason takes the part of the victim. Jason considers what he might do when this happens to him. He could tell the teacher in charge of the lunchroom, but that would make a big scene and Shane would be really mad at him. Jason could push Shane out of line, but that might start a fight. Or Jason could ask Shane, in a calm voice, to go to the end of the line. He decides on the third option. Even if Shane does not obey, Jason will have let Shane know that he is angry, and that will make him feel somewhat better.

Various situations can be explored through role playing with guidance from a teacher who can help students recognize and deal with angry feelings in other than violent ways. Many parents do not know how to channel angry feelings and are pleased to learn from their children about techniques to reduce stress. Whole families practice taking three deep breaths, counting backward slowly, telling themselves to calm down, and thinking nice thoughts when they are provoked and feel like hitting someone.

Even though children are exposed to considerable amounts of violence both in real life and through the media, programs that teach young children ways to solve problems without using violence can help to defuse violent actions in the years ahead. No one is suggesting that such action can solve all of the problems connected with violence, but it can help in the long run, especially if violence prevention programs can address aggression in families, in classrooms, in neighborhoods, and in society as a whole.

One approach to violence prevention is to build self-esteem at an early age. Although theories abound about the complex causes of violence, low self-esteem is a common thread among them. Many people with violent minds have an unfulfilled need for acceptance. They feel incomplete, helpless, and inadequate. In their efforts to achieve dominance, gratification, or whatever they are lacking, these people frequently resort to violence.

Dr. Eugene Aronowitz, Commissioner of Mental Health, Westchester County, New York, thinks that trying to make violent offenders with low self-esteem feel as bad as possible will only make the problem worse. Although their actions must not be condoned and punishment may be necessary, making these individuals, who already feel worthless, feel even worse about themselves may deepen the problem and cause more violent activity. According to Aronowitz, helping violent offenders understand why they act the way they do, developing their motivation and capacity to change their behavior, and helping them make the change, are roles that the mental health system can play in violence prevention.[7]

In contrast to the above approach, experiments with military-style programs use rough treatment of offenders and doses of humiliation in an effort to instill discipline and build character. These programs are popular with authorities because a six-month sentence in "boot camp" costs the government much less than the three-year stint in prison it replaces. This alternative approach relieves the crowding in jails and prisons and gives satisfaction to those who believe in being tough on crime. What effect this will have on reducing future violence among those who participate in such programs remains to be seen.[8]

BATTLING ABUSE AND PREJUDICE

Some violence occurs because old-fashioned ideas of how boys and girls should behave continue to prevail. Many adults were brought up believing that men should control their families with physical force. Women and children were not allowed to think for themselves but were expected to follow the rules set down by the father. If they did not follow them, he was expected to be a "real man" and control them with physical force. This kind of behavior is no longer socially acceptable, but it prevails among many families.

Only a small percentage of abused children and women take refuge in shelters for battered women. Many more continue to suffer violence in their homes. There were 2.4 million reports of child abuse and neglect in 1989, and some of these involved men who control their families through violent means.[9] Men who know how to handle their anger and who respect women and children have volunteered their help at some shelters for battered women and their families. This allows the children to see that there are men who can be gentle and kind.

Another approach to preventing violence is to encourage learning more about people of different backgrounds, sexual preference, and color. In spite of major efforts to reduce discrimination, prejudice continues to be a part of life. Although it accounts for a relatively small part of all violence, it can be especially vicious against victims. Both ethnic and race violence continue to be a fact of life on playgrounds and communities throughout the United States and appears to be on the rise throughout the world.

A rash of violent crimes motivated by prejudice toward sexual preference, race, and religion increased awareness of hate crimes to the point where Congress passed legislation in the spring of 1990 requiring the government to start collecting data on this type of crime, but budget problems have stalled the plans to comply. Some private and local groups have conducted surveys indicating that hate crimes are on the rise. For example, a *Boston Globe* survey of more than twenty cities, states, and private groups suggests a disturbing increase.[10] Hate crimes range from verbal assault to murder. They are instigated by individuals, small groups, and organized hate groups such as the Ku Klux Klan and the neo-Nazis.

96

Researchers exploring the roots of violence against homo-sexuals, among various races, and between ethnic groups suggest that striking out against a hated group makes some people feel good about themselves. In childhood, things are good or bad, and people are either loved or hated. Some adults continue to think this way, seeing their own group as the source of all good. This kind of thinking intensifies their hatred toward those seen as outsiders. Psychologists and psychiatrists suggest that the ag-gression expressed in striking out against a hated group enhances the identity of the actors with their own group, the one they love.

The roots of prejudice often begin at home, when children hear their parents degrading people different from them. This makes young people feel that acts of violence against the "oth-ers" have the approval of their families. They may become more active in guarding their "turf." If someone wanders into a neighborhood where he or she seems out of place, attacks may be so vicious that murder results. For example, an expression of turf violence can be seen in the beating of a twelve-year-old black girl who took a shortcut from her school to a new conve-nience store. A group of whites drove alongside her, asking what she was doing in "their neighborhood." Then they got out of the car, pushed her down, and broke a rib when they kicked her.[11] A more famous example is the murder of Yusef Hawkins, a sixteen-year-old black youth who ventured into a white neighborhood with friends to look for a used car on August 23, 1989. A mob of some thirty white youths, some armed with baseball bats, attacked the black youths. Yusef was killed by these total strangers with two shots from a semiautomatic pistol.

Hatred of gays and lesbians, Jews, and people of color has caused an increase in violence on many college campuses in recent years. This has been responsible for the introduction of new courses that emphasize the cultural values of others, helping to defuse myths about racial differences. Changing the laws to make hate crimes more serious offenses is another effort to curb violent hate crimes. But many of the attitudes that breed this violence were embedded in children while they were growing up, making it difficult to break the cycle of hate.

In hard times, people increasingly need to affirm a sense of their own value. As frustrations build over their own problems, they are more likely to lash out at those they consider different. Devaluing others elevates the self. Sometimes people in groups get carried away with the mood of the crowd and do things they would consider wrong under normal circumstances.

Hate crimes are based mainly on lack of information about others. For example, many people believe that drug use is much higher among blacks than among whites, but according to *Law Enforcement News,* every study that measures drug use by ethnicity or race shows that whites, not blacks, are the dominant users of cocaine and crack. In 1988, the ratio of white to black users was 7 to 1.[12] Whites do buy many of their drugs in predominantly black areas where there is much violence over turf. But the demand for cocaine or crack is driven by a white-dominated consumer market.[13]

Another widely believed myth is that violence occurs mostly between people of different races, but in reality, 80 percent of homicides occur between members of the same race. Young black men run the greatest risk for death and injury from violence. Their homicide rate is six to twelve times higher than the national rate.[14]

STEPS TO COMBAT VIOLENCE

Although the problem of violence in drug-infested communities appears to have worsened as the social forces that held many communities together have dwindled, millions of Americans are now actively involved in neighborhood crime watch programs. Many strong-willed mothers, grandparents, social agencies, and church groups are taking vigilant action. They are fighting back as individuals and as part of community crusades, by reporting drug sales and in a variety of other creative ways. The conditions they live in are foreign to middle-class people, much as the mainstream economy is foreign to many poor black children.[15]

Also, vocational services for teens can dissuade them from becoming involved in dangerous, violent, illegitimate economies.[16]

Nonetheless, many of today's adolescents find themselves disconnected from stable and extended families and community support, unable to find a job with decent wages, and increasingly reliant on peers. For teens in troubled or distressed communities, all of these negative forces are apt to be magnified. Those driven to violence are often loners, teens who have no anchor with people who care. They feel that society's rules do not apply to them; they are mistrustful, secretive, and unable to moderate their anger. These young people need to feel connected to the community and to be given hope that they can be in control of their lives. They need to be encouraged to care for others and to get involved in their communities.[17]

For some children, exposure to serious violence is a problem that influences their behavior later in life. As many as several thousand children in the United States may witness a parent's murder. Many more may discover the victim of a rape or the body of someone (usually a family member) who has attempted or completed suicide. Several million children witness the abuse of one parent by another each year, and millions more witness the abuse of their brothers and sisters. These children have nightmares about violence and often reenact particular scenes and repeat similar themes while at play. Their development can be seriously affected in a way that later leads to violent behavior. Dr. Robert S. Pynoos, director of the Program in Trauma, Violence, and Sudden Bereavement at the UCLA School of Medicine, points out that mental health professionals must develop treatment programs for these children at an early stage in their lives.[18]

The attacks and killings that receive the most attention from the media and public today are not typical incidents of violence. If we are serious about reducing violence, we must attend to the less sensational, daily incidents that take place outside the television spotlights. Since the majority of homicides occur between two young men of the same race who know each other, who have been drinking, and one of whom is carrying a weapon, the issue of guns is an important one. The availability of weapons and their relationship to violent crime is the topic of whole books. (See *Gun Control* by Robert E. Long in the bibliography.)

Although there is much disagreement about the subject of gun control, few dispute the connection between large numbers of guns and an increase in violent crime. A loaded gun kept in the home for the owner's protection is 118 times more likely to kill a family member or friend than an intruder. Awareness of such issues can help to prevent violence.[19]

A further decrease in drug use is another aim of those trying to reduce the amount of violence in today's society. Many studies show that drug use has been decreasing and continues to decline overall.[20] The first evidence from research that drug prevention programs can curtail the use of cocaine by adolescents was announced by federal health officials on June 1, 1990. There has been a downward trend in drug use among high school students nationwide, but this is the first data to be made available on the impact of prevention programs.

Federal money for fighting drugs has been heavily geared toward largely unsuccessful law enforcement programs to reduce the availability of drugs. Dr. Louis W. Sullivan, head of the Department of Health and Human Services, said that this study of drug abuse prevention programs strengthens the point that drug abuse prevention is our front line of offense in reducing the nation's demand for illicit drugs.[21]

The roots of youth violence are tangled and numerous, and attempts to prevent it must come from many fronts. Becoming aware of the causes and extent of violence and of some of the approaches to dealing with it is just a beginning. Solutions to the problem of violence prevention come from researchers, individuals, communities, justice systems, educators, and numerous others working toward the same goal: decreasing the amount of violence. Although there is no quick fix, there are steps in the right direction.

GLOSSARY

Aggression: verbal, physical, or symbolic attack; hostility.

Alcohol: most commonly used drug.

Amphetamines: group of synthetic stimulants that increase behavioral activity and produce a feeling of euphoria.

Amygdala: an almond-shaped structure, part of the limbic brain that plays a role in the emotions.

Antisocial personality disorder: lack of ability to adhere to social values or to form close ties to other people, callous indifference to others, inability to feel guilt or learn from experience or punishment, repeated conflict with society, impulsiveness, and irresponsibility, with a tendency to blame others.

Assault: unlawful infliction or attempted infliction of injury on another person. Aggravated assault includes the use of a deadly or dangerous weapon.

Cerebellum: the portion of the hindbrain that regulates and coordinates motor balance and behavior.

Cerebral cortex: outer layer of the brain that is responsible for the control and integration of movement and the senses, as well as memory, language, and thought.

Character disorder: see Personality disorders.

Cocaine: drug made from coca leaves that produces a high. It is addictive and can cause death in allergic individuals.

Crack: highly addictive, smokable form of cocaine that produces a brief high.

Delusion: a false belief that is firmly held, despite obvious proof to the contrary, and that is not shared by other members of one's culture.

Depressant: any drug that inhibits nervous system functioning and behavioral activity.

Dissociative disorder: sudden, temporary alteration in normal consciousness—for example, amnesia after experiencing trauma or multiple personality disorder, a state in which behaviors suggestive of two or more personalities are exhibited by the same person, as if two groups of mental processes existed without connection.

Ego-syntonic: aspects of a person's thoughts, attitudes, and behavior that are acceptable to his or her total personality.

Epilepsy: a brain disorder causing convulsions and/or other nervous system disturbances.

Euphoria: a warm, joyous feeling; heightened sense of well-being.

Explosive personality: a person who usually appears normal but shows intense and often undirected aggression during periods of explosive rage and violent reaction to the environment.

Genetic coding: the arrangement of genes, the units of heredity that determine individual characteristics of an organism.

Hallucination: a sensory perception in the absence of any actual stimulus; for example, hearing voices or seeing visions.

Heroin: a derivative of morphine that is injected, sniffed, or smoked. Users develop tolerance. Heroin is both physically and psychologically addictive.

Homicide: causing the death of another person without legal justification or excuse.

Hypothalamus: a peanut sized structure near the base of the brain that regulates a variety of functions, including heart rate, hunger, sex drive and sleep.

Insanity: old term for mental disorder, now used only as a legal term.

Insanity defense: legal concept that a person cannot be convicted of a crime if he or she lacks criminal responsibility by reason of insanity.

Limbic system: a lower center of the brain involved in emotional behavior and the visceral changes associated with emotion.

Lobotomy: a psychosurgical procedure involving the severing of nerves between the frontal lobes and the thalamus or hypothalamus and the limbic system: also called leucotomy.

Marijuana: a commonly used drug with highly subjective effects; wrongly accused of producing widespread violent behavior.

Mass murder: the killing of four or more victims at one location.

Mental illness or mental disorder: illness with psychological or behavioral symptoms and/or impairment in functioning, due to social, psychological, physical, chemical, biological or genetic causes, or a combination of these.

Methadone: a synthetic narcotic used to treat heroin addicts that eliminates withdrawal symptoms and the need for heroin; addictive.

National Crime Survey: statistics on crime reported to police plus those not reported to police; uses periodic interviews of victims.

Paranoid schizophrenia: a type of the serious mental disorder, schizophrenia, characterized by suspiciousness and that typically involves delusions of persecution or grandeur, sometimes accompanied by hallucinations.

PCP (phencyclidine): a drug producing a wide variety of effects, including dissociation and heightened sensitivity to outside stimuli. The latter may be associated with violent behavior.

Personality: the way in which a person thinks, feels, and behaves; a style or pattern of relation to the environment that each person evolves as he or she develops.

Personality disorders: deeply ingrained, inflexible, maladaptive patterns of thinking, relating to others, or behaving, which cause either distress or impairment in functioning.

Polydrug use: the use of more than one mind drug at a time to enhance the effect or as the result of combinations found in street drugs that are diluted with cheaper drugs. For example, some drugs sold as pure amphetamines often contain PCP.

Psychopath: *see* Antisocial personality.

Psychosis: a serious mental disorder in which there is severe impairment of a person's ability to recognize reality, to think, communicate, and behave appropriately. Abnormal thinking may include delusions and hallucinations.

Psychosurgery: brain surgery to alleviate psychopathological conditions.

Rape: unlawful sexual intercourse by force and without legal or factual consent.

Robbery: theft, including physical threat or attack.

Role playing: a skit in which actors play the parts of other people to practice for real life situations.

Schizophrenia: a disorder characterized by disturbances in thinking. Some of the symptoms may be delusions, hallucinations, regression, social withdrawal, and impairment of functioning.

Serial murder: the killing of several victims in three or more separate events.

Sociopath: *see* Antisocial personality.

Spree murders: killings at two or more locations, with almost no time break between murders, as the result of a single event.

Stereotactic surgery: a procedure in which tiny electrodes are implanted in the brain and used to destroy a very small number of cells in a precisely determined area.

Uniform Crime Reports: an index that evaluates changes in the volume of crime; annual reports that show trends in eight major categories; counts only crimes coming to the attention of the police, those against persons twelve years old and older, and against their households; based on statistics contributed by states and local law enforcement agencies.

Violent crime: events such as homicide, rape, and assault that may result in injury to a person. Robbery is also considered a violent crime because it involves the use of threat or force against a person.

NOTES

CHAPTER 1: YOUTH AND VIOLENCE

1. "Youth Guilty of Setting Fire to Boy in Brooklyn Cellar," *New York Times,* Oct. 25, 1990.

2. "Number of Killings Soars in Big Cities Across U.S.," *New York Times,* July 17, 1989.

3. *Report to the Nation on Crime and Justice,* Bureau of Justice Statistics (Washington, D.C.: U.S. Department of Justice 1988) p. 26.

4. National Center for Health Statistics, 1988.

5. *Crime in the United States,* Uniform Crime Reports (Washington, D.C.: U.S. Department of Justice, 1989), pp. 9, 16, 24.

6. Ibid, p. 6.

7. John A. Calhoun, *Violence, Youth and a Way Out* (Washington, D.C.: National Crime Prevention Council, 1988), unpaged.

8. Testimony of Congressman Dan Coats, before the House Select Committee on Children, Youth and Families, Mar. 9, 1988, p. 8.

9. Testimony of John A. Calhoun, executive director of the National Crime Prevention Council, before the House Select Committee on Children, Youth and Families, Mar. 9, 1988, pp. 104–105.

10. "When Rage Explodes, Brain Damage May Be the Cause," *New York Times,* Aug. 7, 1990.

11. "Teenagers Who Refuse to Join Drug Dealers," *New York Times,* Jan. 4, 1990.

12. *Report to the Nation on Crime and Justice,* p. 42.

13. Material taken from *New York Times,* March and April 1989.

14. "U.S. Is by Far the Homicide Capital of the Industrialized Nations," *New York Times,* June 27, 1990.

15. NBC News Special, "Bad Girls," Aug. 30, 1990.

16. "U.S. Is by Far the Homicide Capital of the Industrialized Nations," *New York Times,* June 27, 1990.

CHAPTER 2: PROBING THE BIOLOGICAL ROOTS OF
  VIOLENCE

1. Charles Hampden-Turner, *Maps of the Mind* (New York: Macmillan, 1981), p. 80.

2. Vernon H. Mark and Frank R. Ervin, *Violence and the Brain* (New York: Harper and Row, 1970), pp. 14–16.

3. Hampden-Turner, p. 80.

4. Mark and Ervin, p. 58.

5. Ronald H. Bailey, *The Role of the Brain* (New York: Time-Life Books, 1975), p. 125.

6. James Q. Wilson, and Richard J. Herrnstein, *Crime and Human Nature* (New York: Simon and Schuster, 1985), pp. 102–103.

7. Ronald H. Bailey, *Violence and Aggression* (New York: Time-Life Books, 1976), p. 13.

8. "Eight Student Nurses Slain in Chicago Dormitory," *New York Times,* July 15, 1966.

9. *The Economist,* July 22, 1989, p. 72.

10. Richard M. Restak, *The Mind* (New York: Bantam Books, 1988), p. 280.

11. Jose M. R. Delgado, *Physical Control of the Mind* (New York: Harper and Row, 1969), p. 88.

12. Alan W. Scheflin and Edward M. Opton, Jr., *The Mind Manipulators* (New York: Paddington Press, 1978), p. 340.

13. Richard M. Restak, *The Brain: The Last Frontier* (Garden City, N.Y.: Doubleday, 1979), p. 124.

14. Richard M. Restak, *The Brain* (New York: Bantam Books, 1984), p. 128.

15. Ibid., p. 16.

16. Restak, *The Brain,* p. 130.

17. Ashley Montagu, *Man and Aggression,* 2nd ed. (New York: Oxford University Press, 1973), p. 139ff.
18. Material taken from Montagu, *Man and Aggression.*
19. Knud Larson, *Aggression: Myths and Models* (Chicago: Nelson-Hall, 1976), p. 46.
20. P. B. Medawar and J. S. Medawar, *Aristotle to Zoos* (Cambridge, Mass.: Harvard University Press, 1983), p. 4.
21. *U.S. News and World Report,* Apr. 13, 1987, p. 59.
22. *Fact Sheet,* Centers for Disease Control, 1986.
23. Testimony of Carl S. Bell, M.D., appearing on behalf of the American Psychiatric Association before House Select Committee on Children, Youth and Families, May 16, 1989, p. 16.
24. *The Economist,* July 22, 1989, p. 72.

CHAPTER 3: LEARNING TO BE VIOLENT
1. Testimony of Shawn Grant before the House Select Committee on Children, Youth and Families, Mar. 9, 1988.
2. Neil Alan Wiener and Marvin E. Wolfgang. *Pathways to Criminal Violence.* Newbury Park, CA: Sage Publications, 1989, p. 137.
3. Ibid, p. 147.
4. "Elder Abuse on Rise," *Christian Science Monitor,* Sept. 27, 1990.
5. Psychology Today, Sept. 1987, page 25.
6. "Elder Abuse on Rise," *Christian Science Monitor,* Sept. 27, 1990.
7. "Murders by Husbands Rise Despite Publicity," *Christian Science Monitor,* Feb. 6, 1990.
8. Crime and Crime Prevention Statistics, National Crime Prevention Council, revised Oct. 1988.
9. "Murders by Husbands Rise Despite Publicity," *Christian Science Monitor,* Feb. 6, 1990.
10. Ronald H. Bailey, *Violence and Aggression* (New York: Time-Life Books), 1976, pp. 47–48, 51–53.
11. Gilda Berger, *Violence and the Media* (New York: Franklin Watts, 1989), p. 66.
12. Ibid, p. 72.
13. Ibid, pp. 71–72.
14. Hyde, Margaret O., *Crime and Justice in Our Time* (New York: Franklin Watts, 1980), pp. 37–38.
15. Berger, Gilda, *Violence and the Media* (New York: Franklin Watts, 1989), p. 144.

16. Berger, Gilda, *Violence and Sports* (New York: Franklin Watts, 1990), pp. 114–115.

CHAPTER 4: DRUGS AND THE VIOLENT MIND

1. Sheigla Murphy and Marsha Rosenbaum, investigators for Women and Cocaine, letter to the editor, *New York Times,* Jan. 13, 1989.
2. Harvard Medical School, *Mental Health News Letter,* Feb. 1987.
3. Denis J. Madden and John R. Lion, *Rage, Hate, Assault and Other Forms of Violence* (New York: Spectrum Publications, 1976), p. 100.
4. Testimony of John A. Carver, Esq. before the House Select Committee on Children, Youth and Families, Mar. 9, 1988, p. 51.
5. *Report to the Nation on Crime and Justice,* 2nd ed. (Washington, D.C.: U.S. Department of Justice, 1988), p. 51.
6. Marguerite Saunders, director, Division of Alcoholism and Alcohol Abuse, New York State, letter to the editor, *New York Times,* Oct. 17, 1989.
7. Richard C. Allen et al., *Readings in Law and Psychiatry* (Baltimore: Johns Hopkins Press, 1968), p. 315.
8. *Report to the Nation on Crime and Justice,* p. 50.
9. *Drugs of Abuse,* Washington, D.C.: U.S. Department of Justice, Drug Enforcement Administration, 1988, p. 50.
10. *PCP. Phencyclidine Abuse: An Appraisal,* Research Monograph 21, National Institute of Drug Abuse, 1978, pp. 242–243, 278–279, 282.
11. Edward M. Brecher, *Licit and Illicit Drugs* (Boston: Little, Brown, 1972), p. 414.
12. *Clinical Psychiatry News,* Apr. 1990, p. 6.
13. Arnold M. Washton and Mark S. Gold, eds., *Cocaine: A Clinician's Handbook* (New York: Guilford Press, 1987), p. 29.
14. J. Reid Meloy, *The Psychopathic Mind: Origins, Dynamics and Treatment* (Northvale, N.J.: Aronson, 1988), pp. 296–299.
15. Testimony of John Carver before the House Select Committee on Children, Youth and Families, Mar. 9, 1988, p. 50.
16. *U.S. News and World Report,* Mar. 5, 1990, p. 24.
17. *The Economist,* Apr. 1, 1989, p. 28.
18. "Crack's Toll on Babies Is Emotional," *New York Times,* Sept. 17, 1989.
19. *Newsweek,* Feb. 12, 1990, pp. 62–63.
20. "5% of Newborn Babies May Need Drug Care in New York by 1995," *New York Times,* Oct. 8, 1989.

21. Testimony of Karl Zinsmeister before the House Select Committee on Children, Youth and Families, May 16, 1989, p. 118.

CHAPTER 5: DOWN THESE MEAN STREETS

1. Ken Auletta, The Underclass (New York: Random House, 1982), p. 99.
2. American Health, Nov. 1990, p. 55.
3. "High Crime in 1980's Attributed to Drugs," Boston Globe, Aug. 5, 1990.
4. Statement of George Miller, before House Select Committee on Children, Youth and Families, Mar. 9, 1988, p. 8.
5. Catalyst, National Crime Prevention Council, Nov. 1989, p. 3.
6. "Mom Gets Life; Sold Girl," USA Today, Aug. 30, 1989.
7. Charles V. Wetli, "Fatal Reactions," in Arnold S. Washton and Mark S. Gold, eds., Cocaine: A Clinician's Handbook (New York: Guilford Press, 1987), p. 50.
8. Controlling Drug Abuse: A Status Report, Special Report from the Controller General of the United States, (GAO/GGD 88-39), p. 2; and Alcohol, Drugs and Driving, Connecticut State Police Office of Safety Education, 1990, unpaged.
9. "Despite Its Promises of Riches, the Crack Trade Seldom Pays," New York Times, Nov. 26, 1989.
10. "13 Year Old Shot to Death," New York Times, June 3, 1989.
11. Testimony of Ismael Huerta before House Select Committee on Children, Youth and Families, Mar. 9, 1988, pp. 15–18.
12. "The Summer's Violence," Christian Science Monitor, Sept. 14, 1990.
13. "Police to Escort Students in Subway Cars," New York Times, May 4, 1990.
14. "Violence Rises in Elementary Schools," New York Times, May 23, 1990
15. "Schools See Empty Desks on Halloween," New York Times, Nov. 2, 1989.
16. "Police and Schools Try to Head Off Halloween Trouble," New York Times, Oct. 31, 1990.
17. Carl Taylor, Dangerous Society (East Lansing, Mich.: Michigan State University Press, 1989)
18. "The Heartbreak That Is New York," U.S. News and World Report, Sept. 24, 1990, p. 37.

19. Testimony of Howard Spivak, M.D., deputy commissioner of Massachusetts Department of Public Health, before House Select Committee on Children, Youth and Families, May 16, 1989, p. 29.

20. *American Health,* Nov. 1990, p. 50.

CHAPTER 6: MURDER: THE ULTIMATE VIOLENCE

1. Colin Wilson, *A Casebook of Murder: The Changing Patterns of Homicidal Killing* (New York: Cowles Book Co., 1969), p. 37.

2. Gerard G. Neuman, Ph.D., *Origins of Human Aggression* (New York: Human Sciences Press, 1987), p. 81.

3. Martin Daly and Margo Wilson, *Homicide* (New York: Aldine de Gruyter, 1988), p. 144.

4. Colin Wilson, *A Criminal History of Mankind* (London: Granada Publishing, 1984), p. 112.

5. Ibid., p. 108.

6. Daly and Wilson, p. 243

7. Ibid., p. 194.

8. Hans Toch, *Violent Men* (Cambridge: Schenkman Publishing Co., 1984), p. 195.

9. Ibid., p. 213.

10. Steven E. Katz, M.D., "The Criminality of the Mentally Ill: A Dangerous Misconception," *Intelligence Reports in Psychiatric Disorders,* December 1985, p. 7.

11. "Facts Belie Public Perception About Insanity Defense," *Clinical Psychiatry News,* Jan. 1989, p. 9.

12. Eugene Revitch, M.D., and Louis B. Schlesinger, Ph.D., *Psychopathology of Homicide* (Springfield, Ill.: Charles C. Thomas, 1981), p. 47.

13. Donald T. Lunde, *Murder and Madness* (San Francisco: San Francisco Book Company, Inc., 1976), p. 87.

14. "Mass Slayings and Toll: McDonald's Biggest Case," *New York Times,* Apr. 25, 1987, p. 9.

15. Jack Levin and James Alan Fox, *Mass Murder* (New York: Plenum Press, 1985), p. 3.

16. Ibid., p. 139.

17. Colin Wilson, *A Casebook of Murder,* p. 109.

18. Ibid., p. 35.

19. Joel Norris, *Serial Killers: The Growing Menace* (New York: Dolphin Doubleday, 1988), p. 19.

20. Ibid., p. 222.

21. Ibid., p. 244.

22. Ibid., p. 204.
23. Revitch and Schlesinger, p. 173.
24. Deborah Cameron and Elizabeth Frazer, *The Lust to Kill* (Oxford, UK: Polity Press, 1987), p. 1.

CHAPTER 7: TROUBLED MINDS, DAMAGED BRAINS, AND PSYCHOSURGERY
1. William S. Fields and William H. Sweet, *Neural Bases of Violence* (St. Louis: Green, 1975), p. 355.
2. Elliot S. Valenstein, *Great and Desperate Cures* (New York: Basic Books, 1986), p. 84.
3. Alan W. Scheflin and Edward M. Opton, *The Mind Manipulators* (New York: Paddington Press, 1978), pp. 245–246.
4. Fields and Sweet, p. 353.
5. Ibid.
6. Valenstein, p. 62.
7. Scheflin and Opton, p. 250.
8. Fields and Sweet, pp. 355–356.
9. Samuel Chavkin, *The Mind Stealers* (Boston: Houghton Mifflin, 1978), p. 2.
10. Valenstein, p. 253.
11. Vernon H. Mark and Frank R. Ervin, *Violence and the Brain* (New York: Harper and Row, 1970), p. 70.
12. Mark and Ervin, p. 148.
13. Chavkin, p. 38.
14. Ibid., p. 2.
15. *Hospital and Community Psychiatry,* Feb. 1990, unpaged reprint.
16. Statistics from fact sheet prepared by the Office of Scientific Information, National Institute of Mental Health, Mar. 1990.
17. Donald T. Lunde, *Murder and Madness* (San Francisco: San Francisco Book Company, 1976), pp. 63–81.
18. William J. Curran et al. *Forensic Psychiatry and Psychology* (Philadelphia: F. A. Davis, 1986), p. 393.
19. Robert D. Hare and Janice Frazelle, "Psychobiological Correlates of Criminal Psychopathy," paper presented at the annual meeting of the American Society of Criminology, Washington, D.C., 1981.
20. Ken Magid and Carole A. McKelvey, *High Risk: Children Without a Conscience* (New York: Bantam Books, 1988), p. 2; and William P. Reid, *The Psychopath* (New York: Brunner/Mazel, 1978), pp. 3–21.

113

21. J. Reid Meloy, *The Psychopathic Mind: Origins, Dynamics and Treatment* (Northvale, N.J.: Jason Aronson, 1988), pp. 41–59.
22. Stanton E. Samenow, *Inside the Criminal Mind* (New York: Times Books, 1984), pp. 95–117.
23. Meloy, *The Psychopathic Mind*, pp. 110–112.
24. Robert D. Hare, *The Psychopathy Checklist* (Vancouver, Canada: University of British Columbia, 1985).

CHAPTER 8: TOWARD A LESS VIOLENT SOCIETY
1. Rollo May, *Power and Innocence: A Search for the Sources of Violence* (New York: W. W. Norton, 1972), pp. 182–183.
2. "Programs Find Adolescents' Use of Cocaine Can Be Curtailed," *New York Times*, June 2, 1990.
3. *U.S. News and World Report*, June 4, 1990, p. 82.
4. John A. Calhoun, *Violence, Youth and a Way Out* (Washington, D.C.: National Crime Prevention Council, 1988), unpaged.
5. Quoted in Glynn R. Owens and J. Barrie Ashcroft, eds., *Violence: A Guide for the Caring Professions* (Dover, N.H.: Crom Helm, 1985), pp. 3–4.
6. *Psychology Today*, Apr. 1975, p. 85.
7. Eugene Aronowitz, *Mental Health and Violence* (New York: Prodest, 1985), pp. 125–126.
8. *Newsweek*, May 22, 1980, p. 42.
9. *The Catalyst*, National Crime Prevention Council, May 1990, p. 2.
10. "Hate Crimes Rise in U.S.," *Boston Globe*, July 29, 1990.
11. *Time*, May 7, 1990, p. 106.
12. *Law Enforcement News*, Mar. 31, 1990, p. 14.
13. Ibid.
14. Testimony of Howard Spivak, M.D., before the House Select Committee on Children, Youth and Families, May 16, 1989, p. 31.
15. *U.S. News and World Report*, Aug. 22, 1988, pp. 49–55.
16. Testimony of Carl C. Bell, M.D., American Psychiatric Association's Committee of Black Psychiatrists, before the House Select Committee on Children, Youth and Families, May 16, 1989, p. 22.
17. Calhoun, *Violence, Youth and a Way Out*.
18. Harvard Medical School, *Mental Health Newsletter*, June 1990, p. 8.
19. Testimony of Carl C. Bell, p. 21.
20. *The Catalyst*, National Crime Prevention Council, Nov. 1989, p. 3.
21. "Programs Find Adolescents' Use of Cocaine Can Be Curtailed," *New York Times*, June 2, 1990.

BIBLIOGRAPHY

Apter, Steven, and Arnold P. Goldstein. *Youth Violence: Programs and Projects.* New York: Pergamon Press, 1986.

Ardrey, Robert, *The Territorial Imperative.* New York: Atheneum, 1966.

Atyeo, Don. *Blood and Guts: Violence in Sports.* New York: Paddington Press, 1979.

Berger, Gilda. *Violence and Drugs.* New York: Franklin Watts, 1988.

―――. *Violence and the Media.* New York: Franklin Watts, 1989.

―――. *Violence and Sports.* New York: Franklin Watts, 1990.

Bode, Janet. *The Voices of Rape.* New York: Franklin Watts, 1990.

Buzawa, Eve S., and Carl G. Buzawa. *Domestic Violence: The Criminal Justice Response.* Newbury Park, Calif.: Sage, 1990.

Campbell, Anne, and John J. Gibbs. *Violent Transactions: The Limits of Personality.* New York: Basil Blackwell, 1986.

Chatlos, Calvin, and Lawrence D. Chilnick. *Crack: What You Should Know about the Cocaine Epidemic.* New York: Putnam, 1987.

115

Chavkin, Samuel. *The Mind Stealers*. Boston: Houghton Mifflin, 1978.

Clarke, James W. *American Assassins: The Darker Side of Politics*. Princeton, N.J.: Princeton University Press, 1982.

Cohen, Alan M. *Kids Out of Control*. Washington, D.C.: Psychiatric Institute of America Press, 1989.

Curran, William J.; A. Louis McGarry, and Saleem A. Shah. *Forensic Psychiatry and Psychology*. Philadelphia: F. A. Davis, 1986.

Dolan, Edward F. *The Insanity Plea*. New York: Franklin Watts, 1984.

Fields, William S., and William H. Sweet, eds. *Neural Bases of Violence*. St. Louis: Green, 1975.

Gelles, Richard J., and Claire P. Cornell. *Intimate Violence in Families*. Newbury Park, Calif.: Sage, 1990.

Godwin, John. *Murder USA: The Ways We Kill Each Other*. New York: Ballantine Books, 1978.

Holmes, Ronald M. *Profiling Violent Crimes*. Newbury Park, Calif.: Sage, 1989.

Holmes, Ronald M., and James DeBurger. *Serial Murder*. Newbury Park, Calif.: Sage, 1988.

Huff, C. Ronald. *Gangs in America: Diffusion, Diversity and Public Policy*. Newbury Park, Calif.: Sage, 1990.

Hyde, Margaret O. *Drug Wars*. New York: Walker and Company, 1990.

Hyde, Margaret O., and Elizabeth H. Forsyth. *Suicide*. New York: Franklin Watts, 1991.

Kramer, Rita. *At a Tender Age: Violent Youth and Criminal Justice*. New York: Henry Holt, 1988.

Levin, Jack, and James A. Fox. *Mass Murder: America's Growing Menace*. New York: Plenum Press, 1985.

Long, Robert E., ed. *Gun Control*. New York: H. H. Wilson, 1989.

Lorenz, Konrad, *On Aggression*. New York: Harcourt Brace, 1966.

Lunde, Donald T. *Murder and Madness*. San Francisco: San Francisco Book Company, 1976.

Madden, Denis J., and John R. Lion. *Rage/Hate/Assault and Other Forms of Violence*. New York: Spectrum, 1976.

Magid, Ken, and Carol McKelvey. *High Risk: Children Without a Conscience*. Golden, Colo.: M and M Publishing, 1987.

May, Rollo, *Power and Innocence: A Search for the Sources of Violence*. New York: W. W. Norton, 1972.

Montagu, Ashley. *Man and Aggression,* 2nd ed. New York: Oxford University Press, 1973.

Neuman, Gerard G. *Origins of Human Aggression*. New York: Human Sciences Press, 1987.

Norris, Joel. *Serial Killers: The Growing Menace*. New York: Doubleday, 1988.

Nuwer, Hank. *Steroids*. New York: Franklin Watts, 1990.

Owens, R. Glynn, and J. Barrie Ashcroft. *Violence: A Guide for the Caring Professions*. Dover, N.H.: Croom Helm, 1985.

Rosenbaum, Dennis P., ed. *Community Crime Prevention*. Beverly Hills, Calif.: Sage, 1986.

Sagan, Carl, *The Dragons of Eden: Speculations on the Evolution of Intelligence*. New York: Random House, 1977.

Schostak, John. *Schooling the Violent Imagination*. New York: Routledge and Kegan Paul, 1986.

Storr, Anthony. *Human Destructiveness*. New York: William Morrow, 1972.

U.S. House of Representatives. Hearings before the Select Committee on Children, Youth and Families, March 9, 1988, May 16, 1989, and June 15, 1989.

Valenstein, Elliot. *Great and Desperate Cures*. New York: Basic, 1986.

Weber, George H. *Child Menders*. Beverly Hills, Calif.: Sage, 1979.

Weiner, Neil A., and Marvin E. Wolfgang, eds. *Pathways to Criminal Violence*. Newbury Park, Calif.: Sage, 1989.

Weisberg, Lynne W., and Rosalie Greenberg. *When Acting Out Isn't Acting: Understanding Child and Adolescent Temper, Anger and Behavior Disorders*. Washington, D.C.: PIA Press, 1988.

Wilson, Colin. *A Casebook of Murder: The Changing Patterns of Homicidal Killings.* New York: Cowles, 1969.

Wilson, James Q., and Richard J. Herrnstein. *Crime and Human Nature.* New York: Simon and Schuster, 1985.

FOR FURTHER INFORMATION

Clearinghouse on Child Abuse and Neglect and Family
    Violence Information
P.O. Box 1182
Washington, DC 20013

Drugs and Crime Data Center Clearinghouse
1600 Research Boulevard
Rockville, MD 20850

Family Violence and Sexual Assault
Center for Women's Policy Studies
2000 P Street, NW, Suite 508
Washington, DC 20036

Justice Statistics Clearinghouse
P.O. Box 6000
Rockville, MD 20850

Juvenile Justice Clearinghouse
P.O. Box 6000
Rockville, MD 20850

National Coalition on Domestic Violence
P.O. Box 15127
Washington, DC 20003

National Clearinghouse for Alcohol and Drug Information
P.O. Box 2345
Rockville, MD 20852

National Crime Prevention Council
1700 K Street NW, Second Floor
Washington, DC 20006

National Criminal Justice Reference Service
Box 6000
Rockville, MD 20850

National Organization for Victim Assistance
717 D Street NW, Suite 200
Washington, DC 20004

INDEX

ABOUT THE AUTHORS

Margaret O. Hyde is the award-winning author of over seventy books for young people. Among the books she has written for Franklin Watts are *The Rights of the Victim* and *Missing Children*, which she co-wrote with her son Lawrence E. Hyde. In addition to writing and teaching, she has served as a science consultant to the Lincoln School of Teachers College at Columbia University in New York City. She lives in Old Saybrook, Connecticut.

Elizabeth Held Forsyth, M.D., a child psychiatrist, has collaborated with Miss Hyde on several books. A graduate of the Yale University School of Medicine, she has worked as a clinical instructor in psychiatry at the University of Vermont College of Medicine and has served as a psychiatric consultant for the Burlington, Vermont public school system. Dr. Forsyth resides in Phoenix, Arizona.

Ms. Hyde and Dr. Forsyth's most recent book for Franklin Watts is a second revised edition of *Suicide*, which was praised by *School Library Journal* as "a first-rate revision of a first-rate book."